A FAMILY AFFAIR

Helping Families Cope with
Mental Illness: A Guide
for the Professions

Report No. 119

A Family Affair

Helping Families Cope with Mental Illness: A Guide for the Professions

Formulated by the
Committee on Psychiatry and the Community

Group for the Advancement of Psychiatry

BRUNNER/MAZEL *Publishers* • New York

Library of Congress Cataloging-in-Publication Data
A Family affair : helping families cope with mental
   illness.

   (Report ; no. 119)
   Includes bibliographies and index.
   1. Mentally ill—Family relationships. 2. Adjustment
(Psychology) 3. Readership surveys. 4. Van Buren,
Abigail, 1918-   . I. Talbott, John A.
II. Group for the Advancement of Psychiatry. Committee
on Psychiatry and Community. III. Title: Helping
families cope with mental illness. IV. Series:
Report (Group for the Advancement of Psychiatry) ;
no. 119. [DNLM: 1. Adaptation, Psychological.
2. Family. 3. Mental Disorders—psychology.
W1 RE209BR no. 119 / WM 100 F198]

Library of Congress Cataloging-in-Publication Data

RC321.G7 no.119 [RC455.4.F3]   661.89 s   86–18866
ISBN 0–87630–444–7   [362.2'4]
ISBN 0–87630–443-9 (pbk.)

Copyright © 1986 by the Group for the Advancement of Psychiatry

Published by
BRUNNER/MAZEL, INC.
19 Union Square West
New York, New York 10003

MANUFACTURED IN THE UNITED STATES OF AMERICA

STATEMENT OF PURPOSE

THE GROUP FOR THE ADVANCEMENT OF PSYCHIATRY has a membership of approximately 300 psychiatrists, most of whom are organized in the form of a number of working committees. These committees direct their efforts toward the study of various aspects of psychiatry and the application of this knowledge to the fields of mental health and human relations.

Collaboration with specialists in other disciplines has been and is one of GAP's working principles. Since the formation of GAP in 1946 its members have worked closely with such other specialists as anthropologists, biologists, economists, statisticians, educators, lawyers, nurses, psychologists, sociologists, social workers, and experts in mass communication, philosophy, and semantics. GAP envisages a continuing program of work according to the following aims:

1. To collect and appraise significant data in the fields of psychiatry, mental health, and human relations;
2. To reevaluate old concepts and to develop and test new ones;
3. To apply the knowledge thus obtained for the promotion of mental health and good human relations.

GAP is an independent group, and its reports represent the composite findings and opinions of its members only, guided by its many consultants.

A FAMILY AFFAIR: HELPING FAMILIES COPE WITH MENTAL ILLNESS: A GUIDE FOR THE PROFESSIONS was formulated by the Committee on Psychiatry and the Community. The members of this committee are listed on page vii. The members of the other GAP committees, as well as additional membership categories and current and past officers of GAP, are listed on pp. 95–102.

CONTENTS

FOREWORD

This is a book about how families try to deal with mentally ill relatives and what they need in order to continue in their heroic tasks. The reports of their experiences, conveyed in the stark and honest language of alternating despair and courage, bridge the distance between the two groups of caregivers: families and professionals. This book is an important contribution. It gives legitimacy to the family experience, provides insights for the practitioners, and evokes human responses to these puzzling illnesses. These human responses, I believe, are as necessary as the application of scientific principles in the treatment of these conditions.

I am grateful for the unique opportunity I had to serve as an Ittleson Consultant to the Committee on Psychiatry and the Community of the Group for the Advancement of Psychiatry in this endeavor. I shall never forget the day when these psychiatrists listened in stunned silence to the reading of the letters received from family members of the mentally ill. The visible effects of those letters on the committee members provided a rare moment of communion with me and a better understanding of my experiences and those of other families. I hope that readers of this book will share their compassion and concern.

SHIRLEY STARR
Past President, National Alliance
for the Mentally Ill

INTRODUCTION

A generation ago the state hospital was accepted as the only appropriate place for the care of mental patients whose families could not afford private hospitalization. Home care was seldom considered; instead hospitalization relieved the family of the burden as well as the opportunity of caring for the mentally ill member. A frequent result of mental hospital care, as the months and years went on, was the loss of the patient's ties to the family.

In recent years better understanding of mental illness (including the importance of maintaining the patient's family ties), new medications and other treatment methods, the emergence of new public attitudes toward the rights of patients, and the rising costs of hospital care have all contributed to the reduction of the duration of hospitalization and the rapid "deinstitutionalization" or release of patients from our mental hospitals. Care in the home and the community has increased with deinstitutionalization and with the development of locally-based treatment methods that seek, if possible, to avoid hospitalization altogether. In a study of long-term severely disabled patients in the community in California, for instance, more than 50 percent were living with relatives (Lamb & Goertzel, 1977). And in states with less in-migration, as many as two-thirds may return to their families (Minkoff, 1978).

As part of this redirection of mental health services, new responsibilities and new burdens have been placed on the families of the mentally ill. The nature and extent of these responsibilities and burdens and the problems they have produced have been to some extent obscured by the emphasis usually given to the individual deinstitutionalized patient, particularly the patient without a family. We believe, however, that more attention needs to be paid to the families with whom many, if not most, of these patients live, both for their own mental health and because they represent the human milieu within which the patient's rehabilitation does or does not take place.

In order to learn more about these problems from their sources, we asked for help from Abigail Van Buren, author of the internationally syndicated newspaper column "Dear Abby." She generously agreed to our request and inserted the following note in her column in June, 1982:

> **Confidential to My Readers:** *If a member of your family has been diagnosed as "mentally ill" and is living at home, please write and tell me what problems this has created for you. Your firsthand experiences are needed for an important mental health study.*

The firsthand experiences provided by Dear Abby's readers form the basis of this report, whose purpose is to inform all those concerned in any way with the care of the mentally ill about the impact of mental illness on the family. The letters speak more powerfully for the families than we as professionals ever could. As Dear Abby says:

> The more than 450 letters that I received in reply to this single brief inquiry eloquently tell the tragic story of what life too often is like with a mentally ill person in the family. The immense grief of these families over lost dreams and hopes for a promising child or beloved spouse and the suffering caused by a mentally ill parent or sibling are cruelly aggravated by undeserved guilt and shame, by alienation from friends and neighbors, by severe financial drain, and by the paucity of desperately needed resources. Many respondents

said that they did not receive the support they needed from either the helping professions or from psychiatric and social institutions.

The message is loud and clear: The family of the chronically mentally ill person cannot carry such responsibility alone. This insight was recognized and emphasized by Dorothea Dix more than a century ago. It is even more important in today's complex world. Because families alone are unable to meet the overwhelming demands, mentally disturbed patients are spilling into our streets and into jails, where their presence creates even greater problems for themselves and for their communities. Families need help. They need information and communication; they need resources for the treatment, care, and rehabilitation of their loved ones; they need financial assistance; and they need periodic respite from the 24-hour responsibility, day after day, as well as from worry over the unpredictable behavior of their mentally ill family members.

My profound gratitude to all who responded to my inquiry by sharing their experiences—their anguish as well as their courage. I hope that their cries for help will be heard, and the recommendations of the authors of this Report will be acted upon by those who have the power, the knowledge, and the ability to reduce the suffering caused by one of our nation's foremost health and social problems.

The respondents related to "Dear Abby" as if she were a close personal friend; they knew that she would safeguard their anonymity and respect their viewpoints. We therefore believe the letters have a special credibility. We recognize, however, that the family members who wrote these letters are not representative of all families of the mentally ill. They came only from those families who read "Dear Abby," who could write easily about their situation, and who took the time to respond. Virtually all of the letters spoke of a seriously ill family member who had required hospital care, and not about a relative with less severe mental illness. Furthermore, since "Dear Abby" specifically asked families to tell her about the "problems" they encountered living with a mentally ill relative, families without problems did not respond. Our goal was not to determine what proportion of such families had problems; instead we sought a greater understanding of the nature of the problems that do exist, out of which will come recommendations for their alleviation.

We have used the letters or excerpts from the letters in as close to their original form as possible. To ensure absolute confidentiality we have disguised any data which might identify the source. Those letters which specifically requested a response from "Dear Abby" or indicated a need for more information were individually answered by "Dear Abby" with assistance from the GAP Committee on Psychiatry and the Community.

A FAMILY AFFAIR

Helping Families Cope with
Mental Illness: A Guide
for the Professions

1

THE FAMILY CRIES FOR HELP

Dear Abby,

With heart hurting, throat choked, tears close—but also with such a relief (which is so complete only another in the same situation could understand)—we placed our 26-year-old son in a community home for the mentally ill today.

Sam was a normal, intelligent, considerate and ambitious young boy until he became ill. To put a date on when this began is almost impossible, but looking back I can remember some—but very few—questions about the ideas which now possess him. No amount of logic changes these ideas; even written proof lasts only a short time. Whether Sam used drugs to make uneasy feelings bearable or whether the drugs caused the unbearable illness is not known.

We have four children. Albert completed four years at a State College (sometimes with straight As) and plans to do graduate work. Sam is next. Joanne graduated from high school and Cynthia is going into 10th grade. My husband is a maintenance supervisor. He can do just about anything, from fixing plumbing to repairing necklaces for a little old lady. I am a secretary.

Sam had a paper route at age 9—got himself up in the morning and off in rain or snow. He did his collecting and saved his money. Then he started working summers packing fruit. At 16 he worked part-time in a factory. This job he lost because he laid down on the cement floor and went to sleep. There were probably other incidents but this is the one he blames. He earned a pilot's license at 17. He was active in sports, football and basketball; girls liked him and he had a pleasing personality.

Sam now lives in his own world most of the time. He is not violent, but of course this behavior could be undependable. Because we don't have money for private care he spent three years in state mental hospitals. He has to take his medication which I fear is not good for him and still he does not get better.

What kind of future does he have? He wants so much just to be married, have a job, a home and a family.

Sam's illness is so hard because we love who he was and feel so bad about what has happened to him. My husband gets angry and thinks he should be able to control what he says and does; he doesn't think Sam tries hard. Albert is a good big brother but Sam's company is not desirable among his friends, especially girls. Joanne went through a bad time at school as a result of her embarrassment. Cynthia is too young to really understand and gets upset by the bad habits or actions. She loves him but is irritated. I cry a lot, pray and try to realize that our mental hospitals are full of people—but why "my Sam"? I am angry because nothing seems to help.

One reads in the paper about the many awful things done by mental patients and you know that the public's fear is understandable—but can't they do a little more to make Sam feel better about himself? I would be so happy to do anything that might help anyone like "my Sam" and in the doing perhaps gain more insight and some peace of mind for my family.

This letter poignantly describes the thoughts and feelings of many families of the mentally ill. The family, concerned, loving and caring, has tried to provide essential support and a protective setting, but the bitterness and discouragement are evident in the mother's words.

In some cases, years of upset and turmoil precede the full recognition that a family member is suffering from emotional illness. In other cases, lack of understanding and sometimes denial, avoidance, and distortion prevent families from acknowledging that there is something the matter. Once this family faced the initial episode, its members were helpless to cope with it. Perhaps if a professional had been available to work with Sam and his family, either separately or together, at the onset of his illness, the family might have understood the illness better and might have been able to place it in perspective. Such support would have depended on Sam's willingness to work with a professional and his agreement to have appropriate material shared with the family; in places where early intervention has been available, the downward course of conditions like Sam's has been reversed or leveled off in many cases.

We hear that Sam spent three years in a state mental hospital and has returned to his family. Sam's mother believes he is not getting better, and questions whether medication is good for her son. Both Sam and his parents need to understand the risks and side effects, as well as the dosage and benefits, from the prescription of these medications. This kind of information is available to patients and families in many but by no means all settings; where it is not available, the treatment regimen is much more difficult to maintain.

Each of the family members has reacted to the catastrophe of Sam's psychosis. His father believes that Sam can control himself—he appears to be denying the extent of his sons's illness. Sam's older brother and younger sister have experienced shame and embarrassment with their friends and classmates. The youngest sister is confused; she does not understand what is happening. Thus, Sam's illness has had significant emotional effects on each family member.

Although Sam is fortunate to have a family that has stuck with him through the various phases of his illness, his presence at home has been demoralizing. The whole family life has changed as a result of the mental illness of one member. Without help in situations like this, family relationships can become not just strained but perhaps ruptured. Yet the professional support that can help families like Sam's adapt to his condition and his continued presence in the home is all too often not available.

Sam's family has had to give up the effort to keep him at home. A mother of another 26-year-old mentally ill man has given up virtually everything in her life to take care of him.

> My son, who should be on his own but cannot function alone, has caused me to take tranquilizers (when in fact he was the one who needed medication), has caused me to miss days at work, has disrupted our family living, and has even been the underlying cause of a divorce between myself and his father.
>
> My son is expensive, he is excessive about everything from alcohol, drugs, tea and coffee and tobacco to the use of air conditioning, water, all utilities (you should see my phone bills for the past eight or nine months). You name it and he goes to extremes with his use of it—exercise, health foods, alcohol, pills, falling in love, getting religion. Whatever he does, it is all or nothing. I cannot sleep at night; he has nothing to do during the day, so he stays awake most nights, not making a lot of noise, but always just enough noise to prevent me from sleeping soundly. I must work to support myself; I am 58 years old and need *some* sleep. His sister and brothers do not like to be in his company; they seldom come to visit.
>
> Even though my 26-year-old is physically healthy, he cannot do anything for me like cutting the grass or planting a tree. It never enters his mind that he could help around the house. He is in a world of his own, and even though he is by nature a kind and compassionate individual, his illness keeps him thinking only of himself. Explaining to him that consideration

and thoughtfulness towards other people are an indication of good mental health has thus far done no good to motivate him.

My social life is nil. If a man should become interested in me he would soon learn that I am bad news because I have a "problem" son.

In short, life with a mental patient can be frustrating, exhausting, heartbreaking as it has been all the years I was trying to raise him, with two younger children. I suspect that a lot of your readers who have such glowing remarks about life with an ill or retarded child are really trying to hide their true feelings.

This mother's life revolves around the patient and his illness; he is a noose around her neck. Unable to be dispassionate about someone she loves, lacking information about his problems and without any apparent support in the management of her son, she is trapped in her situation.

In some cases, the enormity and complexity of the task of helping family members deal with an emotionally ill relative require more than just counseling, as is graphically illustrated in this wife's description of her husband's illness.

My husband was declared mentally ill several years ago and I have been his "guardian" ever since. He has been in and out of institutions more times than I can count. When he is at home, he does not take his medication, begins giving all my things away, uses abusive language, and continually gets so violent that he has sent me to the hospital several times with broken bones and teeth and cuts and bruises. My ill father lives with us and he and my son and other members of the family are all afraid of him.

As soon as the authorities pick him up to put him in the hospital, he gets regulated on his medication which makes him into a model patient, very intelligent, and most cooperative. By the time the judge sees him, he has been on his medicine long enough to appear perfectly normal and I, in my frustration and pain,

appear to be mentally deranged. So they send him
home, slap his wrists and tell him to behave. This has
happened over and over again.

I work as a secretary and when I get home I have
to clean up his messes as well as my father's and do
a day's work when I am already so tired I could drop.
We have had counseling, counseling, and more counseling but the situation still exists. . . . The problems
are too numerous to list and too painful to remember.
. . . so, believe me, I have just about reached the end
of my rope and see no help in sight. I am in poor
health and have no retirement years to look forward
to. If my husband had been institutionalized until he
was well the first time he was hospitalized, my life
would have been at least worth living . . . but, well,
just sign me . . . hopeless.

Although professionals attempted to help this family
through counseling, their efforts were frustrated by the
inability of the mental health and legal systems to require
the patient either to comply with an effective therapeutic
regime or to return to the hospital when his symptoms
returned and before his behavior could have such devastating effects on his family. In such instances, professionals
may have to advocate for the family with the mental health
and legal systems to enable the family to obtain the help
they need.

Letter after letter describes the consequences of a system
which in too few instances provides enough resources for
adequate community care and the assurance of a rapid
return to hospital care if community resources cannot keep
the patient from damaging the family. One of these letters
written by the daughter of a mentally ill mother demon-
strates the painful and confusing experiences of many children of mentally ill parents.

When she first got home, my mother seemed to be
all right and my father went to work. My sister and

I were going to school and she wouldn't let us go. She started screaming at the window and saying she saw the devil and that the sun was going to explode and it got worse. She started screaming at nothing, waving her arms and banging on the windows. She went into her own world and from then on it was kind of like the mother I used to know was dead. She rarely talked to us and she treated us like we were strangers, but she always fed us and wanted us around. I guess it was her mother instinct. But we couldn't touch her or kiss her and she thought we were possessed. My father used to have to sneak us to school in the mornings when he went to work while she was sleeping at 7:30 in the morning and we would always have to sneak out. If she woke up, she wouldn't let us go. When we got home from school, she would always ask where we were and we would have to lie to her in fear she might come looking for us at school.

In many letters the families plead for understanding. They ask for information about the illness: how it happened, how it should be treated, what are the symptoms and signs, what part the family has played in causing it, and how the family can help. A letter written by a young lady about her mentally ill brother tells of her confusion and her search for enlightenment.

This has been a real tragedy for our family. My brother is so intelligent and such a fine person. I do not understand how he became so ill. I do not understand the illness at all. I have been given several reasons for the cause—the death of our father, brain cells that don't connect, a chemical imbalance in the brain, etc. Also, he has a blood clot in his brain. But, none of the answers seem very satisfactory. I read articles on mental illness in the newspapers and magazines, but my questions never seem to be answered. How can a person who was "normal" for years become so ill? Is research being done in the mental health field? If so,

where? My brother has said he would gladly be a
patient at a research center. We do not know where
any are. Why isn't there more information to the public
on mental illness like there is on cancer and heart
disease? I've read that there are more people in hospitals with mental illness than there are with cancer
and heart disease combined.

It is true that many of the answers to the questions that
relatives ask may not be "very satisfactory." But in communities in which counseling for relatives of the mentally
ill is available, families have the opportunity to share their
confusion, their guilt, and their anger, even if there are no
definitive answers. Without such opportunities, they are left
with no one to turn to.

Each of these letters illustrates some of the dilemmas and
frustrations of the families of mentally ill patients living at
home. Many of these families are trying to cope, day after
day, with a mentally ill individual who has trouble working,
holding jobs, forming adequate relationships with people,
and performing simple tasks of everyday living. They try
to cope with a person who shows such profound behavioral
disturbances as odd mannerisms, irrational outbursts, withdrawal, or peculiar rituals. They must deal with the patient's
distorted thinking or perception, such as delusions or hallucinations, or with his periods of elation or depression.
The patient's biological functions, his eating, sleeping, bowel
and bladder habits, may also be affected. Antisocial behavior
may be part of the picture. And all these characteristics are
likely to persist for long periods of time, may well become
worse as time goes on, and even may be lifelong.

So it is hardly surprising that families require support to
cope with the severe problems associated with mental illness.
The goal of the Report is to help families obtain this support
by strengthening the ability of professional caregivers to
collaborate effectively with these families in caring for the
severely mentally ill.

In the next chapter (Chapter 2), we shall use the letters

to Dear Abby to describe the family's response to the onset of the illness. The first step for the family is often the most difficult and painful: to acknowledge that there is an illness. After the initial shock and recognition, the family must begin to put the illness in some kind of perspective. The letters demonstrate that this process is accompanied by a whole range of emotional responses by individual family members, including a sense of loss, guilt, shame, fear of violence, disgust with the mentally ill, resentment, and sometimes anger. Furthermore, the impact of mental illness goes well beyond the identified patient. The balance within the whole family unit is often dramatically changed by the illness of one of its members. The mental illness of a son or daughter has an impact on the parents' marriage and on the other children. When an adult spouse is ill, the marriage and the parent-child relationships are affected.

In Chapter 3 we describe how the family has to cope with treatment and care systems as well as with the legal and political systems, which all too often present obstacles to adequate treatment. Problems posed by a patient's right to treatment and right to refuse treatment, and concerns about the cost of care and insurance must be addressed.

We shall suggest in Chapter 4 that family members often do not find psychiatrists or other mental health professionals as helpful as they could be and sometimes find them antagonistic and unduly critical. Professionals often are reluctant to work with seriously ill chronic mental patients, and it appears from the letters that some professionals lack preparation and skills for dealing with the task. We discuss some possible reasons for the limited availability of professional support to the families of the mentally ill.

In the final chapter (Chapter 5), we shall review the problems presented and offer some specific techniques and strategies for dealing with them. We hope to illustrate how professionals and families can be more effective collaborators, and how through this collaboration some of the pain and burden of caring for the mentally ill can be ameliorated.

2

THE FAMILY TRIES TO COME TO TERMS WITH MENTAL ILLNESS

The recognition and acknowledgment of the fact that a relative has become mentally ill is the first painful task that confronts each member of the patient's family. Our focus in this chapter is on the nature of the individual and highly personal responses to this task.

If the illness is sudden and dramatic in its onset, all the members of the family are forced, despite their unpreparedness, to an immediate awareness that something is radically wrong. When she was only eight, this little girl's world was turned upside down by the eruption of her mother's psychosis:

> One day while my mother was cooking dinner, she asked my father if he heard noises or people talking, but he told her she must be tired and to go to bed early. That same night about two a.m. she woke us all up and said that the people upstairs were Communists and were going to kill all of us, and she started to get really hysterical. She tried to jump out the window and take me and my sister with her, so my father tried to restrain her and calmed her down. The scary part about all of this was that me and my sister didn't know what to believe. My mother was so scared and so convincing in what she was saying that I could tell even my father was a little confused. She took a

13

pipe and was going to try and kill everyone upstairs to defend herself, but my father told her that it would be best to just leave the apartment. My mother was so frightened and scared about the thought that they were waiting outside for her that my father got the neighbor next door to help calm her down because she liked and trusted him, and we all huddled together down the stairs to the garage; my mother had a pipe in her hands all the time we went down the stairs. We got to the car, and my father took her to General Hospital and they gave her a shot to calm her down and released her. They told my father to take her to the family doctor, and we did. She was diagnosed as being paranoid schizophrenic, and it was recommended that she be institutionalized for an indefinite period of time.

If the onset of the illness is more gradual, it may take longer for the family to recognize the problem. This father describes the slow dawning of his awareness that his son was indeed mentally ill:

The greatest problem has been to understand what was unfolding and how to handle the problem. As a professional I had only textbook information about mental illness until I went through living with it for several years. I reread the books, listened to our professional advisors, and then we did the best we knew how to do, playing it from day to day until the storm cloud had gradually passed. When Teddy was seven, we realized he was hyperactive and did not do well in school. When he reached the age of 12, and after I had read an article on the subject, I realized that he had minimal brain dysfunction and was not lazy, not deliberately unstudious, and was acting in a consistent pattern. When he was 27, I realized that he was showing signs of mania. Then I realized he had had periods of depression and periods of experiencing peculiar, unwanted and unpleasant thoughts. Finally I realized he was mentally ill. Again, as at the age of 12, my whole attitude toward him changed, knowing that he was sick rather than just lacking maturity.

The initial shock of recognition that a family member has a serious mental illness is a painful and difficult experience. For most families it is only the beginning of a long and arduous journey. Occasionally, a psychotic illness is self-limited and remits after a relatively brief period, leaving few or no sequelae in its wake, but most patients and their families are not so fortunate and are forced to recognize that mental illness can be a chronic, fluctuating, disabling and disagreeable condition. This second recognition, the recognition of chronicity, usually becomes apparent after the initial episode has moderated and the patient is sent home from the hospital, improved but still clearly compromised by signs and symptoms that foretell the problems still to be faced. Family members vary in the time it takes them to come to terms with this painful fact, but ultimately they must accept their fate and shape their lives accordingly. As one person comments:

> During my husband's psychotic state I was busy just living from one part of the day to the next; now that his condition is somewhat stabilized, I am concerned with the prognosis. Since his illness is chronic, things are not very hopeful.

With more show of emotion, another wife exclaims:

> Suddenly your whole life changes!! I was numb from the realization that this was happening to the one I love, and you are so at a loss as to what to do to help. Your life becomes lonely and confusing, and you are almost like a prisoner in your own home. And it is constant.

Both of these relatives show us their anticipation of the

long and tedious task ahead of them. They will soon learn in intimate and painful detail the nature of the problems with which they will have to deal and will enter their personal purgatory of tormenting emotions, which one young woman has likened to the pangs of grief:

> The effect this has had upon me has been to take me through a variety of strong emotions, including anger, sadness, guilt (if I were a better wife this wouldn't happen; of course this ain't necessarily so but these feelings come, especially between two a.m. and five a.m.—the sleepless hours), bargaining (with whom?), lashing out, crying for hours, personal depression, and now almost an acceptance that this is the way things are, and they must be borne. In fact, I recognize all the stages of grief. I have taken hospice training, and can look at this in an almost impersonal way at times, and I've touched them all.

For others, the quality of their experience is almost indescribable.

> How can you put into words what problems a "mental illness" creates for the rest of the family and not just the immediate members? I don't think I have those words. The sadness, the hurt, the living death, the cruelty of the whole situation, and, worst of all—the frustration of not knowing what is best or what to do or how to help—those "words" just scratch the surface. Just as with so many emotional diseases, you have to live it to understand it and to read between the lines.
>
> * * *
>
> It would take volumes *[writes a woman of life with her schizophrenic son]* to tell you what problems it has caused. Our lives are shattered; we live in constant fear. He is admitted to the state hospital time and time again for short periods of time. [He] roams the street. [We are] constantly getting calls from "of-

fended" people. [He] refuses to bathe, get his hair cut, etc. A normal existence for the rest of the family is impossible, and it is taking its emotional toll on the whole lot of us. I see no light—we are a devastated family.

Every relationship within a family system is affected when a mentally ill relative lives at home; everyone's life may be turned upside down.

My father, after standing by my mother all these years (he has shown much more patience and fortitude than the rest of us ever expected), is now a full-blown alcoholic. My sister (now 24, divorced and working as a janitor) quit high school with only one semester to go. By doing that she also gave up a college scholarship which her straight-A average had earned her. She quit school so she could work full-time and get her own apartment. My brother (now 17, unemployed, with a 7th-grade education) was judged in a courtroom at the age of 12 as ungovernable and has steadily gone downhill from there. He has been a runaway, an alcohol and drug abuser, and has several problems with the law.

It is difficult to appreciate fully the suffering that is aroused. Yet mental health professionals must be aware of the anguish even if they cannot completely fathom its intensity; otherwise they will fail to provide the help and support that individual relatives need to make their role as caretakers easier and more effective. In what follows, we shall attempt to delineate as explicitly and systematically as possible the types of problems posed by mentally ill patients for their relatives and the variety of emotional reactions with which the latter respond. Our task is made easier since, despite their diffidence about being able to convey in words the reality of their situation, those who have written about

their plight have often done so with a pungency that cannot
fail to arouse an echoing empathy in the reader.

Even the most mundane aspects of nursing care have their
special impact for the family members, as with this woman
who was responsible for her husband's management and
support.

> Monitoring his behavior for the doctors' informa-
> tion—hours of sleep, pill-taking, motivation, capability
> of performing tasks, guessing his feelings, etc. To be
> sure of real trends and to estimate progress I keep
> notes. (Where do I hide them? He mustn't feel spied
> on. These are real worries.)

Soberly, almost dispassionately, this letter speaks here to
the burden that faces every family with a mentally ill relative
in its midst: The responsibility for the patient's daily clinical
management and welfare rests squarely on the family's shoul-
ders, regardless of their ability to assume it. The relentless
inevitability of this responsibility is perhaps the most oppressing aspect of the onerous load it imposes, but the
burden is compounded by the distressing characteristics of
mental illness and the painful feelings and conflicts it arouses
in the beholder.

Isolation and Loneliness

The bizarre behavior of psychotic patients that has always
made them the objects of mixed fascination and aversion
is particularly difficult for relatives to witness. Not only have
they been forced to watch the painful regression of a previously loving and effective person into the grotesqueness
of madness, but each member of the family soon becomes
aware of a sense of social isolation resulting from the stigma
that is the inevitable partner of mental illness. It is, as one
young woman writes, "a very lonely and frightening time,"
a sentiment that is graphically echoed by the widowed
mother of a schizophrenic son:

> Since I am a widow, I would like very much to reach
> out for friends. However, with my son there, I cannot
> share my home with others. There is a good chance
> he will not be cleaned up. His room is always a mess,
> and he causes untold extra work around the house.
> He is not able to assume his share of responsibilities.
> I understand all this, but outsiders—no matter how
> well informed—do not. As a result, I have become
> isolated and a prisoner in my own home.

For some, the isolation appears to be imposed by forces
beyond their control:

> We have become more and more isolated from friends
> and even from family. Some family members do not
> want to talk about our "problem." We are lonely and
> our existence is strange, for the patient and his parents
> are completely involved with the patient's illness. The
> family atmosphere finally becomes filled with stress to
> the point of being "toxic" for everybody.

For others there is a more actively self-imposed withdrawal
and isolation:

> Neighbors, friends, and even "family" are not com-
> patible with our problems, so we have alienated our-
> selves, until we have become unsociable, irritable, un-
> happy and bitter recluses.

Shame

The sense of social stigma and ostracism is, furthermore,
only compounded when individual family members are dis-
gusted by and ashamed of the behavior of the patient, as
is evident in the following comments—the one by the wife
of a severely depressed man, the other by the mother of a
schizophrenic, regressed daughter:

> [My husband] is obsessed with sin and my supposed

sins in particular. He is also overly concerned about
being poor, to the point where he has dragged out a
burnt piece of toast from the rubbish and insisted that
we eat it. He counts the meatballs for the spaghetti,
allowing only two per person, and he gets very upset
when I want to add a few extra.

*   *   *

I knocked on her bedroom door one day after a long
silence from her room and found her standing in the
center of the room letting urine dribble into a bucket
on the floor, as if this were perfectly normal.

Anxiety and Fear

Perhaps even more difficult for family members to deal
with than the embarrassment over their relatives' bizarreness
is the constant anxiety and fear engendered by the irrationality of patients' behavior. This can be unpredictable,
is often seemingly unmotivated, and at times becomes violent, whether aimed against the patients themselves or at
others.

She made my life hell [wrote a daughter about her
existence with her psychotic mother]. I cannot remember
her ever saying a kind word to me. As far as she was
concerned, everything bad that had ever happened to
her was my fault. I was not allowed to date as a
teenager, not allowed to go to summer camp, sleep
over at girlfriends' houses. I was kept at home. She
worked (when "well") and would come home, retire
to her room not to be seen again till morning. From
about four-and-a-half to twelve I was kept in her room
. . . I have memories of waking up with a pillow held
on my face; locked in a closet; falling out of bed at
night and her pushing the beds together so I couldn't
get out; pushing a bed against the door so I couldn't
get out of the room, etc.

The total loss of privacy and the intrusiveness of the

frightening chaos that often surrounds the mentally ill is well described by a disorganized, distraught and despairing mother:

> Our mail is not safe from Jane. What her warped perception dictates, she wantonly confiscates. Our bank had canceled a business credit card for nonuse two months before I finally found the letter in her room. Many items from Internal Revenue Service have not reached us. I never did find them, but my husband has just concluded three weeks of steady visits to the local IRS offices in efforts to straighten out both business and personal tax questions we never knew the IRS had for us. I have currently arranged to have our mail delivered to a temporary address . . . No papers are safe unless locked up. Therefore, a lock on the sitting-room door, which Jane recently removed with a screwdriver, has been reset less accessibly. She took the door frame apart since then to get in.
>
> Jane has developed fetishes about bathing and personal care. She refuses to shave under her arms, may not shower for a week, and when she does shower, most likely won't use a deodorant. It is most unpleasant to be near her at times. Her attitudes about personal hygiene defy logic. I have found used sanitary napkins on a kitchen counter and urine bottles in my refrigerator. Her room smells most unpleasantly of stale smoke and stale body. She smokes heavily and refuses to air the room or use the air purifier apparatus. Of course, the odor permeates the whole house.
>
> A closed door is no barrier—she may knock or may not knock before coming in. I must dress and undress behind a locked door *if* I want privacy. For quiet to study, I must do the same. None of my appliances are safe from Jane's distorted ideas of their use or care. She has damaged or destroyed my new toaster oven, the automatic coffeemaker, and the clothes washer by overloading and repeatedly washing forbidden items. The lock went on my bedroom door immediately after

a trip to Texas. The last night of that trip, Jane threatened to punch my face and followed me across a motel parking lot with a table knife in her hand. I was frightened enough to employ the young man in the motel office to escort me to my unit, where I locked myself in.

For another mother the bizarre behavior of a schizophrenic son compounded by his unpredictable, compulsive violence made her life intolerable. Violence by a mentally ill patient is particularly frightening because it seems so lacking in motivation.

His last stay in the hospital was ordered by the courts after he had broken into a girl's apartment, hit her over the head with a beer mug and attempted to rape her. That was the last and most serious of a long history of breaking into people's homes. He also had episodes of taking off his clothes and walking naked in public places. [He] hears voices and hallucinates that he only sees his father's image instead of himself when he looks in the mirror. He shouts obscenities at the voices and tells them to stop staring at him. Twice he has shattered his mirror with his fist, and once he threw our kitten off the upstairs balcony.

That mania wedded to irrationality poses special problems is clear from the following:

[My father] goes around singing at the top of his voice, and the songs he sings are crude, to say the least. When he is not singing, he is barking, meowing, or whistling. The noise is nonstop, and it can be torture. When [my mother] gets home from church, he starts calling her a slut and accusing her of having an affair at church. When she goes to the store, he will check the mileage on the car to make sure she has gone where she said she was going. He is jealous of my sister and me and resents any attention my mother pays to us. He calls us names and puts us down, and we do nothing to provoke these attacks. He is also jealous of our pets. My dad chases and harasses all of our animals. He will chase our dogs with the lawnmower until they are exhausted. If they get hot and dig a hole, he will yell at them and threaten to cut their heads off. Last Christmas day he spent the whole day threatening to kill us. He is also fanatical about cleanliness. If you go in the kitchen, as soon as you leave, he rushes in to see if anything is messed up. If one spoon is in the water, he washes it, dries it and puts it up. He has to have the house vacuumed at a certain time every day, or it would ruin his entire day.

The Unrelenting Intrusiveness of Psychotic Behavior

Not only must relatives put up with behavior that is strange, unpredictable and frightening, but they must deal with it 24 hours a day without hope of respite from a burdensome duty that is not to be shirked. There is no relief from the incessant demands; no refuge from the toil of constant giving and caring for the regressed, self-centered dependent patient; no chance to get away, to rest, to be alone, to restore one's inner resources through gratifying one's own needs. The burden often falls on the mother when a son or daughter becomes ill. A woman writes of her son:

Of the eleven days of vacation time taken from my present job, four have been taken by me for my personal pleasure; the others have been taken doing things for him—running him to hospitals, picking him up from hospitals, taking him to the clinic, going downtown to bail him out of jail, taking him to straighten out legal matters—he needs a "keeper," and in this case the keeper is the mother who does not have the time to babysit with him, although he needs looking after.

A sick daughter is equally taxing:

She is very hard to live with—wanting my attention constantly, having to take her riding and being with her almost every night. She is very jealous of my husband for she wants me all to herself. It is hard for me to get out—she wants me to have nothing to do with the neighbors for she is the only one that should count. It is impossible to have friends in the house— rather embarrassing with her watching and scowling at everyone. She gets very upset when her sister comes to town, telling her she is not wanted at the house. We always have to plan ahead when we go out and if we are late getting home she gets very upset. The only way we can go on vacation is putting her in the hospital.

The Family's Lack of Understanding of Mental Illness

The burden of caring is often compounded when family members misunderstand the nature of their relative's illness. Often they see the patient's demandingness and disregard for the rights and needs of others as willful selfishness. They do not realize that these behaviors are an integral part of the illness and that the mentally ill may have little control over their moods and behavior. They may not comprehend that madness listens to neither reason nor reality, and their frustration mounts when the patient fails to respond to their appeals for control, conformity, and concern for the rest of the family. Each of the following parents, from four different families, reflects a painful misinterpretation of psychotic apathy, depression, agitation, and withdrawal.

We would ask him to do a little work around the house, mainly because we thought it was very bad for him to sit around the house with nothing to do. But he would do it, if at all, in a desultory way. He never seemed to see anything to do unless you told him, like a child.

* * *

He has no drive or ambition at all. He works, but never lets us forget how he has to work so hard to support us. Every day we hear it. He bathes once every three weeks and then it is at my insistence because we can't stand his offensive odor any longer. He doesn't do a thing around the house. I "remind" him to take out the trash twice a week, have been for 18 years. He refuses to mow grass, wash the car or anything else that is asked of him.

* * *

No amount of "nagging" can get him to pick up his clothes or keep his room neat. His laundry piles up until there is absolutely nothing left to wear, and then only if I help him. Table manners leave something to be desired, with the gulping of food and dropping bits on the floor and table.

* * *

The only important things are (1) [the patient's] mouth and what goes into it, and (2) money and the material possessions it can buy . . . [the patient's] wants, opinions, and interests are more important than anyone else's.

Anger, Guilt, Sympathy, Compassion, Ambivalence

It is not surprising that families react to their involuntary task with a variety of emotions. A young woman with a manic-depressive husband summed it up vividly and poignantly:

The toll on my emotions is heavy. I often feel that I am on a roller coaster. In the summer my husband is high (manic). He has boundless energy, spends money without good judgment, and gets very irritable with me and my son. In the winter he is suicidal, dependent, lethargic. I get so angry with the treatment I get that I feel like I want to walk out of the door. The only thing that prevents me from doing that is the fact

that I love him and I know what a fine person he is.
I know those are symptoms to the illness he has, and
I keep hoping that we will get a treatment that works
some day.

In the winter he becomes a recluse. He misses a lot
of work. He expresses doom and gloom all the time.
We don't see friends. If I am out of sight for long,
he panics. He regrets all the money he spent in his
high. He gripes at every dollar I spend. Needless to
say, my emotions run from anger at him and the
illness, frustration at being helpless, fear that he will
be successful at suicide, guilt that I might not do the
right thing at the right time, pity for the agony I
know he is experiencing, and love for the man I know
he is when he is normal.

This wife, as we can see, experiences a range of feelings
from fear, to anger, to guilt, with strong urges to run away
and escape the oppressing weight of her responsibility—
negative emotions that are countered by pity and love,
creating in her the irresolution of a vacillating ambivalence.
We have already examined the fearful anxiety that so
often besets the relatives of the emotionally ill. Anger, guilt
and ambivalence are no less frequent and important states
of mind. Anger, in particular, is unavoidable in the face of
the treatment to which patients subject those to whom they
are closest. As one mother wrote:

Anger that this should happen to my child. Anger
that the doctors, despite benefit of the best of minds,
cannot tell me why my child is psychotic. Anger that
I am so completely helpless in doing anything to help
cure my child's illness. Anger that this illness may keep
my only daughter from that which she says she wants
most, a husband and family. Anger that society, though
indeed it has come far, still as a whole looks upon
mental illness with a crippling and painful stigmati-
zation. Anger that, despite the fact that I am now in

therapy, I live with the constant guilt that I may have caused my daughter's illness.

Another older parent commented:

> The therapist at one of our "coping" sessions asked each set of parents what emotions are evoked when we think of our mentally ill son or daughter. The first word which came to my mind was "resentment." It is difficult to feel that we are missing some of the contentment and freedom which many people our age enjoy. We visualize ourselves being tied down indefinitely by our mentally ill son.

The anger expressed by these two parents is somewhat impersonal in its object, being aimed more at an indifferent, neutral fate than at the patient whose illness and behavior are primary causes of the family's woes. In other relatives the resentment is more openly directed at the patient.

> We also resent her because we feel manipulated and used *[wrote a mother of her daughter]*. She has threatened suicide a couple of times, so we feel blackmailed into not upsetting her for fear of what she might do. I feel resentful at being used as a cook, maid, seamstress, etc., with no thanks. She lives like this is a hotel here. I did finally refuse to do her laundry. Now we have shut off her room so it can't be seen.
>
> * * *
>
> I was not physically abused, though she did try to slap me once as a final attempt to make me conform *[commented a daughter about her mother]*. I opened the door just in time for her arm to meet the door's edge. I remember the satisfaction I felt. I hated her; I would pray for forgiveness of my hate.
>
> * * *
>
> I know *[said an exhausted mother]* it is not the state's responsibility to care for your family, and I am plagued very often by thinking I am not a good mother because

I'm tired and wish to abdicate sometimes. It sounds cruel, but I wish I never had Herman. I don't know if there is any love left, and I feel drained emotionally because of him.

In the last two excerpts the writers' resentment and anger are clearly tempered by a sense of guilt at having such feelings toward a sick person whom one ought to love and help. Guilt may result not only from the anger the patient arouses, but from the conviction that one's behavior is making the patient worse, or that one has genetically transmitted the mental illness. All of these factors are poignantly evident in the following excerpts from four different letters:

I guess what makes it worse for me is the guilt I feel. I feel guilty for having been hurt so often that I have a deep resentment inside me. I see my father patiently forgiving and forgetting—loving his wife despite all she's done and accused him of. I see George forgiving his mother all the nightmares she's given him. (He really has had nightmares where he cried out in his sleep). I feel guilty for not being able to forgive as readily as Dad and George do.

*   *   *

My husband and I like to go out and eat occasionally, or stop and have a drink. If we didn't ask our son along, I would feel terribly guilty at the thought of him sitting home alone, and if I did, he would ruin our evening.

*   *   *

The guilt he lays on us is unbelievable because no one knows, not even the doctors, if this illness is transmitted through the parents' genes or if there is a chemical imbalance in the patient.

*   *   *

Our beautiful son took his own life in our home. His diagnosis was "schizophrenia." The torment the parents and the family goes through is unreal. What is this awful thing? How do you treat it? Are we doing the right thing for him? Do the doctors know what they are doing? Should we keep him home? The worst part was trying to understand what was happening. How could this happen to him? To us? To our family? *Always* and *never* stopping asking, "Where did we go wrong? What have we done to our firstborn?" The guilt is unbearable.

Anger and guilt are understandable reactions to a relative's chronic, incapacitating illness. So, too, is the fact that family members often experience anguish from an empathic awareness of the patient's suffering or experience loneliness and isolation in the face of the patient's withdrawal, as the following witnesses attest:

The worst problem that I have had to deal with repeatedly over the years is what do you say when your own mother asks you to help her commit suicide to end her agony? You look in those sad fearful eyes and see the agony, the wanting to be released from this private hell, and say NO, watching the hopelessness and shame sink deeper into the lines of her face. Each time the knife twists deeper into your heart because you want to help her so badly; you want to help her end her agony but by bringing her back to the happy productive life she used to have, not by ending it all.

*   *   *

Two years ago my wife had to be committed twice within two months. Since that time she has withdrawn completely from all social encounters. She does not talk, will not answer the phone or door, and uses notes and her form of sign language to communicate with her immediate family. She tapes her mouth shut except to eat and brush her teeth. She will not eat with the rest of us, but is in reasonably good physical health and exercises in the basement on various pieces of equipment. She keeps house reasonably well and is clean and neat about herself.

With her not talking, any attempt at normal marital relations would come off as being a mechanical act only, so we live as celibates and really find it not too difficult with God's help. The normal sharing of close and happy times is not there, and I can get down sometimes because of this. By this I mean moments important in my life, like when I get a promotion or raise. The joy of going shopping for a new car and picking it out, planning for a long vacation, none of these are possible in her present condition, and I work around them. I think the hardest time is mealtime. I detest eating alone, and find that I eat out a lot.

Despite the magnitude of the burden, many families try to accept it with responsibility, compassion, understanding and love—qualities that shine through the quite matter-of-fact statement of a caring mother.

He was in and out of hospitals for the next three years. When he was released I furnished an apartment for him to live in. Finally, two and a half years ago he announced he couldn't handle living alone and was moving in with me. I had no choice. He is my son, and I love him dearly.

It is not surprising, however, that this selfless altruism is often mixed with feelings of an opposite nature. As one burdened wife put it:

Though I feel that my husband suffers abysmally, and I feel great sympathy for him, I truly believe it is time to give some attention to those of us who are suffering dreadfully through the pain of mental illness in our families.

As this last quotation implies, the response of family members to the sick patient is seldom exclusively caring and loving, or exclusively resentful and rejecting. In many cases, perhaps in most, the family member (like each of the mothers in the following excerpts) is caught in the crossfire of a conflict between these two opposing attitudes and manifests a state of chronic, painful ambivalence.

> He still spends most of his time at home. He yells obscenities at his "voices" and says very sadistic things. I am torn two ways—no one wants him around, so I hesitate to make him go to his apartment, but lately I can't stand the constant hatred and screaming, and I have physically attacked him and thrown him out and told him not to come back until he can be quiet. I'm afraid I'm burned out on the situation, but I will not give up on it. I love him very much. I can't desert him. I many times wish to be free of the ordeal, but never of him even though sometimes I lose control.
>
> * * *
>
> I love my oldest child dearly, but I can't stand to let him live this way. Last week he was living in an alley eating garbage, with little kids throwing bottles at him. . . . If this continues [she commented], I am going to give him a gun and let him kill himself, or else I will do it.

The Parents of the Mentally Ill Person

As the excerpts from the letters have shown, all family members are affected by a mentally ill relative living at home. The specific impacts—on parents and their marriages, or on spouses or siblings, and on children—may differ somewhat. There are differences, too, within categories. Thus, the extent of impact of a child's illness on the parents' marriage will vary with the severity of illness and the strength and resiliency of the parents' marriage. Even in situations where adaptation is relatively successful, the burden of caring for the patient can cause significant marital stress. The loss of privacy, the loss of vacations, the loss of opportunity for the parents simply to enjoy each other's company, all are sources of continual marital stress.

> My husband and I have been unable to take even a weekend vacation together for over three years, something we have treasured doing in the past. We have had to forego that companionship. My husband had to pass up an expense-paid trip to England and my pleasure was tinged with guilt at going without him. Much of the normal middle-age growth and pleasure has been denied us by our daughter's condition.

The couple's sexual relationship can be affected, as well as their capacity for intimacy at every other level.

> There is absolutely no privacy for a husband or wife. My husband is being treated for impotence for the past six months. We exist only as brother and sister. When he arrives home in the evening and after the dinner is over, he immediately falls asleep in front of the TV so he won't have to cope with his son or answer all the questions that I must answer all day.

Often, the stress leads to a deterioration of the marriage and the emergence of hatred and resentment, as the demands of the patient drain the abilities of the couple to support each other.

> The marriage was affected to the point that I hated him (my husband) because he wouldn't try to understand.
>
> *   *   *
>
> My husband and I constantly fight over our schizophrenic son.

The stress can progress to the point where the marriage is destroyed, particularly when one parent, more often the father, is unable to accept the illness. In such cases, the mother-child relationship may prove stronger than the bonds of marriage.

> In our case, my husband felt that nobody in his family could be imperfect and, after years of being secretly ashamed of his own son, left the family. Now, with the other children all gone and living alone with a 28-year-old who is in a world of his own, I can find no opportunity to have a life of my own. It has left me bitter and resentful because his father walked away from his responsibilities. He has begun a new life. He can have normalcy in his everyday living, but I am not allowed the same change; the mother is stuck with the problem.

Other couples can present a more united front, and choose to preserve the marriage by extruding the ill child.

> In our particular case it would have broken up our home if we would have continued to try to maintain our son at home with us.

The Siblings of the Mentally Ill Person

The impact of chronic mental illness on brothers and sisters may be as powerful as it is on parents. Because the siblings are themselves "children" within the parental family system, they may be even more vulnerable to the devastation and pain. As one parent points out:

> Our other children bear scars for a long time from their exposure to the actions of my son—and from having to take a backseat for the child who demands so much of our time, energy and thoughts.

The presence of an ill child also may bring out intrafamily problems far beyond the identified person. This may lead to depression and loss of self-esteem in the siblings. A sibling wrote:

> My parents bought her nice clothes, trying to make
> her feel pretty. They still ignored me. My wardrobe
> fell apart and people started to laugh at me in school,
> I felt "safe" at home where I didn't have to face those
> people. I didn't complain too much about my clothes.
> When I did my mother called me "selfish." I knew
> how she felt. We all lived under a strain. All I ever
> heard about was my older sister. I secretly resented
> it.

Many siblings often feel an intense pressure—from their
parents or within themselves—to be helpful and supportive.
This added responsibility compounds the strain.

> My mother and dad argued a lot. She blamed his side
> of the family, he blamed her side. I felt like I was in
> the middle, torn apart, not knowing how to help. So
> I helped by trying to help with my younger brother
> and sister.
>
> * * *
>
> No matter what she did, getting lost in the shopping
> center, for example, my mother took up for her baby.
> I resented it and hated them both. If I was invited
> to a slumber party, my mother said I could go alone,
> only to change her mind at the last minute. She felt
> that since my sister had nowhere to go, I had to take
> my sister.

The neglect and the added responsibility can lead to
resentment and rage.

> On the surface, I have a generally good relationship
> with my parents, yet I harbor a deep resentment for
> them. I feel that their weakness and gross mishandling
> of my sister caused unnecessary pain and suffering for
> all involved. No parent, in my opinion, has the right
> to keep a child such as my sister at home, when by
> doing so they neglect the mental and physical health
> of other children. Some of her ridiculous quirks are

as follows: Kit (my sister) decided she didn't care for the smell of oranges. Therefore, my brother and I weren't allowed oranges. Kit has a fixation about never having enough of anything. She has in her bedroom three color televisions (so she can watch the three major networks at the same time), three stereos (that also play simultaneously), a 20-year supply of personal toiletries, thousands of records, and dozens of prescription drugs.

About the records—she has the titles of all her records listed. She only plays them in the order they are written. When we were children, I shared a room with her. The records were also mine at the time, but if I wanted to listen to a certain record I sometimes had to wait six months for its turn to come up.

She fancies herself in love with the doctor (aged 72) next door. My two daughters, age five and eleven, are not allowed to visit their grandparents' house because Kit believes they only wish to do so to steal this doctor away from her. My father drinks to excess, my mother has attempted suicide many times, as has my brother, and through it all I have had to be everyone's Rock of Gibraltar. Believe me, I could ramble on forever, for I've only very briefly touched on the surface of the poison within me.

Some siblings respond by withdrawing support or even sympathy, which in turn may elicit considerable anger from the parents. Two mothers write about the impact of a mentally ill child on the other children.

After my son was diagnosed as psychotic, my heart went out to him. He has two other brothers, but he came first because he needed my help. The other two resented him and wouldn't try to understand his condition.

* * *

I am her mother—but she has sisters who are married with children. They have no sympathy for her—think

she is putting a lot of this on. She is often ignored
by them or they manage to be going somewhere when
she wants to visit them. I used to try to plead with
them to help me keep her busy, but I have given up
on that as I'm afraid I have raised selfish daughters
who don't want to be bothered with a mentally ill
sister.

One woman sums up with great sadness and much regret
the effects of her son's schizophrenia:

The mental anguish was terrible! I agonized over my
son's awful condition to the complete sacrifice of my
other sons. From the time he was diagnosed schizophrenic I went out of my mind . . . I went into a
tailspin and suffered a severe depression. I just couldn't
pull myself together. I knew my son would never take
care of himself, he had to live with my husband and
me as he couldn't stand on his own two feet. Finally,
in desperation, my second husband walked out of our
21-year marriage because he couldn't take any more
of my depression. I know my other two sons suffered
the curse of the damned with the social stigma of this
type of illness.

My prayer is that my experience could enlighten
another parent going through a similar experience,
and perhaps could prevent that parent from giving
one son all their attention and concern. I did this to
the abandonment of my other two wonderful sons and
a great husband. I'm president of the "old too soon,
smart too late" club.

The Spouse of the Mentally Ill Person

The marital relationship can be profoundly and permanently
altered by the emotional decompensation of one of the
partners. The mentally ill spouse is unable to hold up his
or her end of the partnership as the level of functioning
deteriorates, while the other spouse is forced into a caretaker
role.

He once was a very intelligent man with a career
ahead. For the past seven years he has been doing
simple clerical work which still puts too much strain
on him. At the present he is on disability and now he
is home 24 hours a day, which is a very hard adjustment
since he does not want to work around the house;
instead, he follows me around and keeps tabs on my
every move. I have had to do all the raising of the
children alone as [with] every other decision.

I no longer look to him for any emotional support,
so I'm not disappointed, but I certainly would never
trust any man again. So in essence the woman is
buried—only the mother is left.

How do spouses survive in such marriages? It is clear
from the letters that almost every spouse faces the question
of whether to remain in the marriage. Most continue to
feel a sense of loyalty or obligation to the partner that leads
them to stay in the relationship in spite of everything:

I [always arrived at] basically the same conclusion—
if you really want any peace of mind and a normal
life, it would probably be best if you left her. Well,
I tried that once and carried such a load of guilt that
I couldn't stay away.

What is financially and emotionally best for the children,
as well as their physical safety, often determines whether
the spouse stays or goes. Some decide to stay:

We have a daughter 27 months old and he is wonderful
with her, but I would be afraid for him to have her
alone for any length of time in case one of his manic
episodes crops up. That is why I probably will stick
with him now. At least I have control over her all the
time, whereas if we divorced he would have her on
weekends or whatever. What a mess.

* * *

I would have divorced him before his first breakdown
if I had a place to go and money for the children. I

feel now that I need his pension and insurance, so
will hang in there.

Others choose divorce:

As I write this, I am trying to get a divorce. He
couldn't accept the fact that he was responsible for
his son and my welfare.

* * *

I left when my life and my children's life became
threatened. It was a hard decision but the best one I
could have made.

Others escape periodically, sometimes leaving the children
behind to cope as well as they can:

She (mother) was diagnosed as paranoid schizophrenic
and it was recommended that she be institutionalized
for an indefinite period of time. But my father didn't
believe in institutions . . . The way my father would
get peace of mind was his vacations and every chance
he got he would like to look around on his own. The
way he would do this was by leaving us in the car.
He would say let's go everyone, but he knew we
wouldn't because we were terribly embarrassed by our
mother' screaming and yelling and if me and my sister
went with my father, my mother would go too! Sometimes for hours we would sit in the car and my mother
would mumble and then she would scream. We would
just be waiting for my father to get back.

The Children of the Mentally Ill Person

The children of a mentally ill parent are probably the most
severely traumatized. Letter after letter recounts the horror
of growing up in such a household, subjected to bizarre,
unpredictable, and often dangerous behavior.

When we were home with [our mother], she could

take us places with her. My sister and I would beg
her to let us stay in the apartment, but she said the
people upstairs would kill us. Sometimes she would
drag us out of the house, and we would walk with
her while she screamed down the streets. This was
the hardest part—the embarrassment. Every day she
would drag us out, and we would walk for miles with
hardly anything to eat, and people would stare, shocked,
at us. I remember one time that really hurt me inside,
and that was when my mother walked us up and down
the same street all night screaming and yelling obscenities, and nobody came to help us.

How are children to cope when the parent they loved
and who loved them, on whom they depended and who
once cared for them, becomes a different person, mired in
a psychotic reality, behaving in ways incomprehensible even
to other adults? How can children make sense of or deal
with this change?

Some children become caught up in their parent's psychotic world.

I realize that many of the things she told me were
her hallucinations or outright lies. But I believed my
mother at the time. Children believe their parents
even when they tell outrageous stories.

Frequently children do not complain or reveal to others
what they are going through, whether from embarrassment,
fear, a desire to protect the ill parent, or simply not realizing
that things could be different. Two children indicate how
they hid their pain.

At school, my performance deteriorated. I broke down
crying in class. I was frequently ridiculed. And my
friends began avoiding me. I was not sent to see a
counselor. My brother, because of his being hospitalized, was getting frequent counseling. Yet I never
complained to my father.

*   *   *

I don't have room here to go into the atrocities she
put us through as children—the swings between brief
periods of loving behavior and wild hateful rages; being
expected to do something one day and punished for
it the next, wearing dirty clothes when she didn't feel
like taking care of us, encouraged to mistreat each
other when she didn't like one of us, being forced to
write letters to dead members of the family apologizing
for some misdeed created in her imagination. Being
children, for some reason we never told anyone about
all this—not even my father, who was gone most of
the time as a community leader. My grandmother saw
enough to know things were not right but was afraid
to do anything because it might make her worse.

Even when it is obvious that the parent's behavior is
bizarre and is traumatizing the children, family and community members may do nothing at all.

I learned a lot after my mother became ill. In a
situation where my mother would scream, people would
react in different ways. Some people would stare in
shock and start mumbling to each other, others (especially younger people) would laugh and mock her,
and still others would look at her and look at us and
look mad or upset. But most people would ignore her
or look down while walking by. Even the police would
ignore us.

In this situation, any sense of self worth or inner strength
is likely to be eroded away, as described by this daughter:

I spent 15 years in therapy trying to undo the damage
done to me as a person. When I left to go to college,
I felt as if I had lived in a box for 12 years. I felt no
one loved me, that I would love no one. I had so
many hang-ups. I felt I had no "person"—a negative
self-image I still fight. The only thing that saved me

was I am an intelligent person and a *strong person* and the psychiatrists have said that is what saved me from freaking out myself.

I wondered many times if *I* was crazy. I could not tell anyone what was happening—for who would believe me? I was brought up to *never* upset mother and to *never* show emotion—not cry, not be angry. In fact to survive I could never let her know she got to me. The one goal I had in life was to get out of that house and to never, ever, be like her.

Looking back, many children discover a legacy of a profound and abiding sense of anger.

And we kids? We are 39, 34, and 29 and we hate her [their mother] so much that we can't look directly at her when we pay her a visit. I visit home less frequently than I would like because I feel an obligation to see her for two hours when I go back. I can't relax when I visit my father or grandmother because the visit with her is looming ahead of me. Now, when we cannot forget, cannot forgive, we are told we should love her because she is sick—we who were raised without compassion are supposed to acquire compassion for her.

As the letters demonstrate, the presence in the family of a relative with chronic mental illness corrodes not only relationships with the mentally ill relative, but also all other relationships within the family. The families not only lose the emotional support of the patient, but often become unable to care for and to understand each other.

3

THE SUPPORT SYSTEMS
SOMETIMES FAIL

In the foregoing chapter, excerpts from letters from family members have dramatized the variety of painful emotions they have experienced when faced with the devastating and often grotesque changes wrought by mental illness. Many of these families are receiving external support and help in carrying the burden of care at home; too many, however, are carrying it alone or with inadequate help.

> Sometimes *[wrote the mother of a schizophrenic son]* I don't care and just want out of this dreadful situation. I just feel like taking a train, plane or bus to anywhere, but I don't. I still love him and want to help, but I could sure do with some help myself sometimes.

The major changes in mental health care brought about by deinstitutionalization have too often failed to provide proper help for patients and their families. Despite all the thought, time and money devoted over the past three decades to improving mental health care, too many relatives of patients who live at home feel alone and unsupported.

> Something must be done for the mentally ill. My heart aches for them. Everyone is supportive of the victims of cancer or heart disease, etc., but the mentally ill person is still an outcast, even in this day and time. The family is usually left alone to handle the burden. I don't know how much more I can bear.

* * *

> The difficulties of living with someone who has no
> job, no friends, no independence, no way to get self
> esteem, no money, no place in the world, are endless.
> Nor can we share our burden with anyone.

They are concerned for the future as well as the present.

> The unsolvable problem of what is to become of our
> son upon our deaths or disability plagues my husband
> and me ceaselessly. State facilities as they now exist
> are unacceptable. Residential care is nonexistent, or
> cost prohibitive, or both. He cannot make it alone,
> and we fear his falling into the hands of uncaring,
> unscrupulous persons. We are currently in the process
> of revising our will to a trust fund which will specify
> that his needs be met after we die, but we can't come
> up with how to furnish him with *people who will love
> him* and care for him. This is our dilemma.

Without adequate support from the larger social system,
these families, locked into caring for a mentally ill relative
seven days and seven nights a week, soon become emotionally and mentally exhausted. The respite provided by
hospitalization is hard to arrange.

> She's been in four or five times. I lose count. But she
> has to DO something violent before we can get her
> committed. Our fear is someday it'll be too late. Mean-
> while, the buildup to the point when she becomes
> violent may take two months to maybe three months.
> All this time we live with this depression. If there
> were some way of being able to give us a break for
> a few weeks through the worst part, it would really
> help.

Furthermore, hospital care often is perceived to be sub-
standard or insufficient.

Hospitals are woefully inadequate in trained staff or facilities. Alcoholics and drug addicts are grouped with other patients, as are homosexuals and sometimes criminals. In the state hospital in our area, our son was made worse by homosexual advances from other patients. The food, cold and unpalatable, was served in a very unappetizing manner by scruffy aides. On occasion our son has been victimized by sadistic aides (not always in state hospitals, this occurred in a very prestigious hospital for which we were paying a premium price). Once a patient attempted to set fire to our son's clothing. So you will be able to comprehend why we choose to keep him home if at all possible.

The rapid release encouraged by deinstitutionalization may be too rapid.

We have found that the hospital dismisses the patient at the very first sign of any remission at all, with only a suggestion that the patient report to his mental health clinic.

On the other hand hospital and follow-up care can work out:

Fortunately, the state hospital kept Helen six months. When she left, she was a new person—it was a miracle! She sold her home and rents a room at the home of a couple who were her friends. She goes to the mental health clinic three days a week and leads a nearly normal life. She had never gotten help on her own until after her last hospital stay. We were told state hospitals were the last place to send someone, which we found totally incorrect. I have the highest regard for the state mental hospital system.

Families are often beset with overwhelming financial problems, especially when they seek help in private facilities.

Financially, my brother has just about been wiped out.

He has spent over $40,000. He has his house left and
that is all. When he is hospitalized, his Blue Cross
policy only pays for 30 days of hospitalization. Sometimes my brother is hospitalized more than that. What
are people supposed to do?

* * *

At this time he was in a private hospital costing a
fortune and before the pensions had started so I had
no income. His family suggested that I sell the house
and use the money to get him well. But at this point,
I realized that he would never be well and that I was
head of the family, so I grew up and did what I knew
was best for the other three of us. I had him trans-
ferred to a VA hospital.

Families who turn to social agencies for financial help
find that it is often difficult to get and is subject to policy
changes and confusing regulations.

Although advertisements indicate that SSI benefits are
readily available, it is very difficult and lengthy to
qualify and remain qualified. If a person doesn't understand the forms or know whom to call, they lose
the benefits. The only way I got the benefit for my
son was to hold a hearing, get lawyers and professionals
to testify. It took a year. He didn't return the infor-
mational card they sent periodically and so the benefits
were dropped and now we are going through the
entire process again.

Some decisions are perceived as arbitrary and insensitive.

The community mental health center psychiatrist in-
forms us he is recommending that welfare discontinue
her disability payments, that she can get a job, although
she must continue her Prolixin shots lest she lapse
into catatonia, although she has not held a job or ever
stayed more than six months in one place, for the last
two years. We are dumbfounded and dismayed.

Many families have heard of community services, but find that they either do not exist in their communities or cannot meet their needs.

> There is no day program for her. For two years she attended one which she liked, but then due to a change of management, I was told she was not progressing fast enough.
>
> * * *
>
> I feel that there should be halfway houses for these people, not the rundown places we see around where people are housed in dirty conditions that are not fit for anyone.
>
> * * *
>
> My son, aged 20, has been in and out of mental wards of hospitals six times in the past four years. Each time the doctors say they have done everything they can to "stabilize" him and that he needs a "sheltered environment." The social workers have spent months trying to find such an environment. They tell us that if my son were a drug addict or alcoholic there would be a place for him, but for the mentally unstable there is no such place in this state, so he is sent home to us.
>
> * * *
>
> We worry about what will become of him when we are dead—the only future we can see for him is living out his life in a mental institution if he is lucky enough to be admitted to one, or in a prison. Society has really done us a disservice by emphasizing "mainstreaming." It means that experts have removed themselves from responsibility, and have left the agony to people who are totally untrained and unprepared to handle the problems of the mentally unstable person.

It is uncommonly cruel to both patients and families to give families no recourse when their mentally ill relatives wander off to live on the streets eating out of garbage cans and/or behave, because of illness, in such a way that they are in and out of jail.

The problems created by restrictive commitment laws complicate still further a painful process for the family. Most families find they can only with great difficulty bring themselves to initiate commitment proceedings in the first place.

> . . . but they urged us to have him committed to a mental institution. If you don't know this, the only course open to accomplish this is by a court order which is beyond comprehension that you could do to your child, until the time comes that there is nothing left for you to do.

Many families clearly describe this power without responsibility (and families' responsibility without power):

> I realize the laws are to guard against families committing people that don't need to be committed. My opinion is if those legislators lived for one year in our house and saw how miserable life can be for those who have to live with the nonviolent schizophrenic— some laws would change.

Perhaps the efforts to establish a "right" to refuse treatment epitomizes the problems created for both patients and their families by some "patients' rights" advocates:

> Our greatest need is for *someone* to apply some sanity to the legal insanity which is choking a caring family, willing (at great sacrifice) to provide what professional care (not incarceration) we can. Our daughter is 26 years old. We have an undisputed diagnosis from five psychiatrists of paranoid schizophrenia. We have been trying for two years through legal channels to get permission to hospitalize her for three months at the finest hospital in New England for trial medication (after which she may return home). We do have per-

manent guardianship of her, but court permission is necessary for medication and hospitalization because she refuses. Her symptoms are inabilities to make rational decisions, yet the law (and the court-appointed young legal eagles) say her decision takes precedence, rather like insisting the unconscious patient must sign her own admission papers or expire where she falls.

The lack of understanding of the needs of both patients and their families among some legislators is due in no small part to the vigorous lobbying by various groups who claim that psychiatrists are out to disenfranchise helpless patients for self-serving reasons. Patients and distraught families have in the past been unable to muster effective political opposition to these groups. We mental health professionals must join with interested and compassionate citizen groups to inform legislators about the destructive implications of misguided mental health laws.

Although many families lay the blame for poor medical care at the doors of the mental health facilities and their professional staffs, some are aware that larger social forces are at least partly responsible. The social legislation designed to protect the rights of patients sets up legal obstacles to proper care and simultaneously places too much responsibility on families; there is currently a tendency to place a greater value on an individual's civil rights than on society's duty to protect its members from harm. Patients as well as families need access to short-term hospitalization during acute crises but current commitment laws make it difficult if not impossible for such "cooling off" periods to be implemented. The families, however, more often than not feel too drained and dispirited to engage in political action which might bring much-needed changes in the social and legal system.

In my opinion legislators and others who formulate mental health laws would do well to consider the plight of *families* of mental patients, and not just the patients themselves. Is it selfish to feel that *I* have a right to live, that other people besides the patient should be given *some* consideration?

* * *

I think the most frustrating thing about dealing with this illness is the inability to get the patient the help he needs. When [my husband] was first hospitalized, I found out how really difficult it is to get a sick person help. He has to want it, and he was in no condition to judge what he wanted or needed. Further, it is apparently the basic nature of a manic-depressive to not see what is happening to himself. The doctor has told him to let someone else judge who can see the onset of symptoms. That does not work, however, because he resists my judgment. Therefore, he has to be suicidal before he will go to a doctor, and even then he goes only after threats of divorce, etc. Needless to say, it is nothing short of hell for me to see the inevitable depression coming and to know that he may well take his own life while I stand helplessly by waiting for him to "want" treatment. I really am frustrated by those laws which protect patients' rights to that degree. I realize that some people have been stuffed into mental hospitals when they did not need to be there, but [I] rather think that the laws have gone overboard in the other direction.

To cope successfully with a mentally ill relative, families need all the support they can get, not only from one another but also from the helping professions, from the mental health system, and from social institutions at large. Without that help and guidance they cannot be expected to undertake the task of caring for their sick relatives.

Deinstitutionalization has served to protect the civil liberties of mental patients, but in the process it has too often subjected patients' families to the tyranny of madness. Too often deinstitutionalization has been implemented without providing the professional support for patients and their families that is essential for the adequate maintenance of the mentally ill outside of mental institutions. If families are to be required to participate in the care of their sick relatives, they must be given the tools to make sure that they can do so effectively.

We shall have more to say in the next chapter about the part that psychiatrists and other mental health personnel can play in helping families to manage sick relatives living at home.

4

THE FAMILY SEEKS HELP

> The largest problem I have encountered is that the professionals will not talk to the family members. When someone you love becomes disturbed, you want very much to help, to keep the lines of communication open and let that person know how much you care. This has become increasingly difficult. These professionals will not acknowledge that what is wrong with my husband is having repercussions through the family. It is indeed a family affair.

Mental health professionals who are aware of the stresses endured by families who are trying to maintain their mentally ill relatives at home recognize the importance of communicating with the family members as well as with the patient. Unfortunately, however, there are many psychiatrists and other mental health professionals who appear neither to sense nor to respond to the needs and problems of these family members.

In the letters Dear Abby received in response to her request specifically for comments on "problems" faced by families living with mentally ill relatives, family members had a good deal to say about the professionals, especially the psychiatrists, with whom they had come into contact. While some commented positively, the majority were highly critical, but because of the nature of the sample, it is impossible to generalize about these experiences. It may be that families who had positive encounters with the mental

health system were less likely to be motivated to respond
to the survey. Nevertheless, the types of difficulties the
families in our sample did describe are certainly not un-
common, and they illustrate the clinical challenges which
must be overcome in order for professionals to work effectively with the families of the chronic mentally ill. In
this chapter, therefore, we will concentrate on the critical
comments the respondents made and then discuss some
possible reasons why professionals may fail to respond adequately to the needs of these families.

How Professionals Are Perceived to Respond

The major criticism in the letters was that families felt
psychiatrists and other mental health professionals did not
communicate sufficiently with family members. Some of
them were convinced that the subsequent treatment of their
relatives suffered accordingly.

> I feel very strongly that an attempt on the part of
> the professionals to communicate with us could have
> saved our family and my husband.

Many families expressed the wish for a psychiatrist with
a sympathetic ear to understand their pain and turmoil. As
one mother said:

> I think the biggest help would be being able to talk
> to someone who knows the heartaches we feel and
> has been through it, or even to sit down with someone
> who understands why I need to cry.

Appropriate communication is a two-way street, involving
listening to families' needs and eliciting information about
the patient as well as feeding back information, advice, and
support. Unfortunately these families often felt ignored by
professionals, and felt that the patient's needs were ac-
knowledged while theirs were not.

My attempts to contact the psychiatrist were met with
no success. I was told my son did not want the doctor
to talk to me, so he would not. If anyone needed some
help and support, it was my husband and me. I still
wonder how we survived.

*   *   *

Always we had the reply that they could not divulge
the nature of his illness since he was past 18, and it
would violate some amendment concerning his rights,
but they urged us to have him committed to a mental
institution.

Some of our respondents not only felt ignored, but were
upset when professionals did not even elicit information
from them. The families felt that their familiarity with the
patient enabled them to provide meaningful information
that they believed could be critical to making the best
treatment plan. The following comments illustrate this view:

The psychiatrists and psychologists in this town may
not yet be willing to listen to what our families have
to offer in regards to mental illness, but they should!
They, too, don't know the answer.

*   *   *

After living with a person who is manic-depressive for
so many years, I can detect very early that trouble is
again brewing weeks before a doctor, who only sees
a patient once a month, can detect it.

Many family members in our sample complained that they
need to receive more information and support than they
get. Information about the patient's illness is almost always
helpful—with symptoms, diagnosis, disease process, treatment, or prognosis. Family members hunger for reliable
information about their afflicted relative.

I was thirsting for knowledge, knowledge that was not
forthcoming from the doctors or the nurses.

*   *   *

Cindy informed us, not the doctor, that she was diagnosed as manic-depressive. I think the private hospital was irresponsible in refusing to discuss Cindy's
case with us and in repeatedly releasing her in the
condition she was in.

Sometimes information is conveyed in unhelpful ways:

Ten psychiatrists, on each seaboard, all connected with
medical schools, made little impression on his condition
with the obvious psychological jargon. We've had no
reliable explanation of how or why.

Specifically, many of the patients' relatives who wrote
letters to us want help with the practical management of
the patient at home. They feel professionals should be:

Providing the family with information as to the degree
of responsibility the patient is able to assume for his/
her life, what behavioral limits can or must be placed
on the patient, the degree of responsibility family
members should take for the ill members care (medication, getting patient out of bed, getting patient
involved in activities, etc.).

They want to know what limits to set, what is and is not
part of the disease, what they should do when threatened
physically or when confronted with bizarre behavior and
poor hygiene, how to deal with suicidal impulses or thoughts,
and how to cope with all manner of everyday situations.
Many felt that this help was not forthcoming. As one family
complains:

No one gives the family guidance on helping their
loved ones, though grudgingly they will allow you to
act as a halfway house when the hospital stay is over.

The most commonly reported practical problem was

whether to continue to keep the relative, often a son, at home or to let him fend for himself (a situation many linked to that experienced by John Hinckley's parents). Comments by three parents, each with a schizophrenic son, illustrate the failure of professionals to provide practical advice or support, particularly when resources for housing are inadequate.

> Psychiatrists have been both helpful and unhelpful. Like John Hinckley's parents, we were advised to lock our son out of the house and let the system handle him. What that really means is that we should send him away, knowing that he will get into trouble and end up in jails for the rest of his life. We cannot condemn a mentally unstable person to that kind of existence. Most of the doctors agree that he needs a structured environment—and that our home is not the place for him, but they can suggest no alternative.
>
> *   *   *
>
> He was in private hospitals for about six years until the money ran out. Since then we have had to deal with the State Hospital, the Mental Health Department, etc., and it has been one great big nightmare. Our son has been abused, neglected, and released from the hospital when he was not able to care for himself. He had to find a place to stay for himself. Invariably he was evicted since he is up at night and sleeps during the day. After several such experiences, we retrieved him and took him home, against advice from the "experts" who tell us that we should never have taken him in, even if it's 20 below zero and he is starving. These humanitarians tell my husband and myself that our son will never get better until we let him fall in the gutter.
>
> *   *   *
>
> [Our son] has been in and out of hospitals for those five years at least six times. Each time it has been advised by doctors that he does not come home, but

no one comes up with any place for him to live, so
he comes home.

Another common practical problem concerns medication.
Compliance with medications is often a problem for mental
patients, and families frequently have little professional support as they attempt to cajole or coerce the patient into
cooperating.

> We have tried everything to get him to take his pills,
> even bribery. After several weeks of bribing him, we
> discovered that he was hiding the pills in his mouth
> and then spitting them out.
>
> * * *
>
> He started to refuse his medication so the doctor put
> him on Prolixin. But he would refuse to go for his
> shots, and then would get to feeling and talking de-
> lusional so he would have to go back to the hospital
> and be put on medication again.

When patients do comply, they may suffer serious side
effects from the medicines. Some families complained that
they were not adequately prepared or informed about the
devastation and danger these side effects could cause.

> Even the most well-intentioned psychiatrist might not
> think to mention some of the side effects of the med-
> icines a mentally ill person takes. Coming into our
> home from work one hot summer evening, I found
> my husband stretched out across the bed, near having
> a heat stroke after working in the yard. How surprised
> I was two years later to find that increased sensitivity
> to sunlight and to heat are known side effects of his
> medicine.

Our respondents plead for support as well as practical
management techniques. Yet, for many support is not forthcoming. Many families in our sample not only feel ignored

but blamed often for causing the illness, as this mother notes:

> The psychiatrist told me that I was responsible for my son's [schizophrenia] since I was the most important figure in his life up until then. This nearly drove me mad, nearly . . . I thought if I could have caused this severe illness I didn't deserve to live.

Others felt that the families—and the patients—may be blamed for the lack of progress when the professionals become frustrated with the patient's failure to respond to treatment, as these two examples illustrate:

> The first overriding problem is the continuing problem (trauma) of having a patient whom NOBODY understands or seems able to help. One of the frustrations is that we, the family, feel that after nine years of dealing with our patient we *know* some of his greatest needs and there seems to be nobody and no place to do the most needed things. I can't tell you how often we have asked the psychiatrists, staffs of wards and hospitals, and WHOMEVER—just to make an effort to give HOPE AND ENCOURAGEMENT to our son. What we got was doctors shuffling medication and endless anger because our son could not fit into programs and be successful. He was blamed for being uncooperative and we were blamed for interfering or being too protective even though there seemed to be nothing to replace our support and care.
>
> * * *
>
> Trips to the state hospital have been completely and totally harmful and destructive. Decisions are made by untrained and unprofessional staff. Doctors are often cast-offs. Patients who do not respond by becoming either very submissive or calmer and more cooperative because of medication cause staff to become defensive and to blame the patient for his lack of progress. Punishment is usually meted out (appar-

ently to make the staff "feel better"), and great suffering ensues for the patient and family.

When family members feel unsupported and unhelped,
it is no surprise that they resent the money they have had
to pay for treatment.

> Had we really accepted the chronicity of his illness
> and the realities of our finite financial resources, we
> might not have made all the financial sacrifices we did.
> But, I'm not even certain of that. Families traditionally
> make enormous sacrifices for sick family members
> when they seek a cure of serious illness. The difference
> between this illness and other illnesses is the issue of
> recovery. Without advice to the contrary, we believed
> that recovery justified sacrifice. Now that we know
> what we know, our anger spills out all over the place.
> We're angry at the psychiatrist who didn't ask us about
> our resources when he suggested two years in an
> expensive private institution without giving us the facts
> of chronicity and relative outcome of treatments. We're
> angry at insurance companies who don't and won't
> insure mental illness even as a catastrophic illness.
> We're angry at a society with enormous medical knowl-
> edge and technology that won't provide adequate care
> for those who can't afford it and for those who can
> no longer afford it.
>
> *   *   *
>
> The cost of our son's illness had added an additional
> stress to all the other stresses of mental illness in a
> family. The end of this insurance coverage and the
> depletion of much of our family's savings meant that
> we were forced to accept the inevitability of his place-
> ment into poorly staffed state institutions for any fur-
> ther needed hospitalizations.

What many of our respondents seem to feel they really
need for the patient and themselves is a psychiatrist for the
whole family. But they found few psychiatrists who will

provide competent and compassionate long-term treatment to chronic patients and their families. As one family member put it:

> In my opinion getting a good psychiatrist is the chief problem when a person diagnosed as mentally ill lives at home. It took six years to find my husband's present doctor. We encountered many psychiatrists who would treat well-behaved outpatients but almost none who maintain both a hospital practice for psychotic patients and a private practice for improved patients, routine medication checkup and/or therapy. Of those doctors who did treat psychotics, some were examples of the medical field at its worst: lack of genuine concern for the patient, little or no follow-up care after hospitalization, exorbitant cost for in-hospital treatment. The doctor who currently sees my husband does have a grueling hospital private office practice and is a kind person as well. He is willing to provide treatment over a long period of time, years if necessary. I know that he is the exception, not the rule.

Why Professionals Are Perceived as Unhelpful

The indictment of the mental health profession by many families of the mentally ill in their letters to "Dear Abby" is profoundly disturbing. As we have noted, the extent of the alienation from the mental health profession felt by so many families cannot be ignored. Why is it that psychiatrists are perceived as so unhelpful to families? Some families may be too distressed and upset to recognize the value of the help that is genuinely offered. Many families are also frustrated with and angry at psychiatrists because of the limitations in our ability (and in that of the mental health system in general) to help chronic patients. Yet, many of the complaints voiced in the letters *are* valid, and we must then look for the causes. Why are competent "family psychiatrists" for chronic mental illness "the exception, not the rule?" Why are presumably competent professionals so often perceived by the families of the chronically mental ill as behaving in such unhelpful and untherapeutic ways?

The answers to these questions are complex. It seems clear from the letters, from various studies, and from our own experience as clinicians that working with chronic patients is often more difficult and frustrating than working with "less ill persons," and that working with the families of chronic patients often seems, at least at first glance, more demanding than working with the patients alone. As one of the letter writers observes:

> It is so much easier to deal with less ill persons or neurotics or "families with problems of living" than with those who are afflicted with this terrible, little understood illness.

Meyerson (1978) observed that "mental health professionals generally view treating chronic mental patients as an unrewarding, frustrating experience" and Stern and Minkoff (1979) and Holden and Lewine (1982) report similar findings. In a recent study of professionals' attitudes toward the chronically mentally ill, Mirabi et al. (1985) observe that "85% of the respondents agreed that the chronic mentally ill are not a preferred population to treat, with 55% moderately or strongly agreeing that most clinicians prefer to avoid contact with such patients . . . 63% of the respondents felt that there were not satisfying professional rewards in treating this population, and . . . 59% felt that clinicians received insufficient cooperation from the families of chronic patients."

Other deterrents which tend to discourage psychiatrists from working with these patients and their families include affective barriers, training deficits, and lack of community support. Each of these deterrents will be discussed in the remaining pages of this chapter.

Affective Barriers

As clinicians, we react to chronic patients and their families with strong feelings of our own, which often create barriers to effective intervention. When we work with psychotic patients, professional training does not protect us from experiencing some of the same feelings of fear, guilt, frustration, despair and anger that family members experience. Psychosis can be a terrifying experience for the clinician as well as for the patient and the patient's family. Thus, in order to work with psychotic patients clinicians may keep them at a distance by treating the "disease," not the person, or by focusing on medication rather than on day-to-day living.

When chronicity is added to psychosis, the clinician's need for distance may become even greater. Chronicity challenges our "wish to cure" and our sense of competence and control, so that recognizing the poor prognosis for some of our patients' illnesses means acknowledging our own helplessness. Thus, professionals may be less effective in helping patients because we need to protect ourselves from their pain. We may encourage short-term improvements to "see results," while avoiding the commitment to lifelong care. We need improvement to satisfy our own sense of success, and unfortunately we sometimes blame the patient when he fails to improve. As a result, work with chronic patients often becomes frustrating, and we cope with our frustration by experiencing these patients as "draining," "boring," or "overdependent." It is hardly surprising, therefore, that many, if not most, clinicians find reasons to avoid patients with chronic illness and focus instead on "less ill" people, who are easier to talk with, to understand and to treat.

The same kinds of affective barriers color the psychiatrist's clinical relationship with the patient's family. As the letters clearly state, families want mental health professionals to listen to them empathically, to engage them as allies, and to provide them with emotional support and practical advice. Professionals want families to be supportive and helpful, as the study by Mirabi et al. (1985) indicates, but unfortunately negative attitudes on both sides can interfere with effective collaboration. When confronted with the pain, anger and despair of mental illness, both professionals and families may react to one another—more or less unconsciously—by creating distance instead of encouraging closeness and cooperation. Most clinicians face difficulties when working with these families, and at times have failed to provide families with the support they needed and deserved, because their feelings have gotten in the way.

The feelings that "get in the way" of clinicians working with the families of chronic patients can be divided into five categories.

First, lack of personal experience with mental illness in their own families may make it difficult for clinicians to validate the pain experienced by the patient's family. Clinicians may, therefore, misunderstand the family's perspective, and fail to appreciate the legitimacy of the family's anger, despair, and desperate concern.

Second, many clinicians may recognize that their training has not prepared them to be truly helpful to families in dealing with chronic patients. They don't know what to say or how to help in response to the family's questions, and they fail to realize the considerable comfort and help they can provide. Consequently, rather than forming an alliance with the family, these clinicians may simply avoid the family and its needs. Clinicians may also fail to understand how little families really know about mental illness at the onset, and how much information they need throughout the entire course of the patient's illness.

Third, many clinicians experience chronic patients as extremely needy and draining—they are very sick, usually disabled, and improvement comes slowly with frequent setbacks. When asked to deal with the family's needs as well as the patient's, clinicians may feel overwhelmed. Rather than perceiving the family as a potential ally which could make their work easier, clinicians may feel hopelessly out-numbered. In order to protect themselves, they "draw the line" by excluding the family from treatment.

Fourth, some clinicians may have an especially difficult time empathizing with families who either are overprotective or are expressing negative feelings about the patient. These may be feelings that clinicians are repressing in themselves in order to maintain a therapeutic stance. The family then becomes viewed as the "enemy" of the patient, the clinician, and the treatment. Rather than supporting the family in resolving its negative feelings and developing more adaptive approaches, these clinicians may blame the family for the patient's illness, for the patient's failure to progress, or for "sabotaging the treatment." Thus, a clinician may instruct the family to be tough with the patient by "kicking him out," as if the patient's chronic dependency were due to the family's overindulgence rather than to the mental illness. Such efforts to "protect" the patient from the family may prevent the clinician from involving the family in finding adaptive solutions for coping with the patient and the illness.

Finally, many clinicians feel very stressed by the demands of the role of "family psychiatrist" for the families of the chronically mentally ill. This is a relatively new role for them and may require more activity, more directiveness, and fewer boundaries than the more familiar role of "psy-chotherapist" or even "family psychotherapist." For ex-ample, the "family psychiatrist" must often weigh the fam-ily's legitimate need for involvement and information against the patient's right to confidentiality and trust. This is a real clinical conflict that requires careful consideration as to how to balance the needs of the parents against the desiderata of therapy with the patient.

In addition, the "family psychiatrist" must objectively assess the family's assets and liabilities with regard to how family processes may influence the course of a family member's illness. At the same time the clinician must exercise extreme caution to maintain a non-blaming and supportive stance toward the family. Anxiety stirred up by these new demands may lead the clinician to cling to more traditional approaches that keep families at arm's length.

We suspect that all clinicians experience at least some of these feelings to varying degrees in working with the families of chronic patients. We have found, however, that clinicians who have adequate training and support in working with chronic patients and families can usually learn to recognize and overcome these affective barriers. We cannot overemphasize the importance to clinicians engaged in this type of care of working within a system that provides them the necessary collegial support. Unfortunately, as we shall discuss in the next section, training in this area is often not adequate, and otherwise well-trained clinicians lack adequate skills for this work.

Training Deficits

Several authors have commented on the failure of many current professional training programs in mental health adequately to address the development of skills for working with the chronic mentally ill and their families (see White & Bennett, 1981; Nielsen, Stein & Talbott, 1981; Mirabi et al., 1985). They have called attention to factors which they believe contribute significantly to this failure:

1. *Lack of Specific Curriculum:* There are few applicable publications and few recognized teachers for teaching a comprehensive clinical approach to chronic mental illness. In many settings, trainees must adapt teaching, theory, and supervision better suited for work with "less ill" patients to their work with chronic patients, often with frustrating results.

2. *Lack of Education in Biopsychosocial Integration:* Many
   training programs fail to integrate the biological and
   psychosocial aspects of treatment of the chronic
   patient. To the best of our current knowledge, the
   cornerstone of the clinical understanding of chronic
   patients and their families is that chronic mental
   illness is derived largely from a biological predisposition (Gottesman & Shields, 1972; Rosenthal, et.
   al, 1971; Kety, et al. 1976; Cadoret, 1978), while
   psychosocial factors contribute to the emergence and
   the course of the illness. Although most clinical work
   with psychotic patients uses biologic forms of intervention to treat symptoms, this type of intervention
   should be combined with a wide range of psychosocial interventions to help patients and families
   learn to adapt and cope with the experiences of the
   illness, perhaps over the course of a lifetime. If,
   however, the importance of this integrated theoretical perspective is not sufficiently emphasized,
   trainees may be drawn into one particular "pure"
   therapeutic or theoretical track. As a result some
   trainees may become biologically-oriented experts
   in psychopharmacology without learning the skills
   to help patients and families to learn to cope, while
   others may become psychodynamically-oriented psy-
   chotherapists, again without appreciating the need
   to involve the family in the on-going process of
   adaptation.

   Seventy-three percent of the respondents in the
   study by Mirabi et al. (1985) felt that patients are
   too often treated by a single therapeutic regimen
   when they need a combination of treatment strategies.

3. *Lack of Adequate Supervision:* Most training programs
   have few, if any, senior teachers who are experienced in working with the chronically mentally and

their families. Trainees often are supervised in their work with chronic patients by clinicians who work primarily with neurotic or acute psychotic patients. As a result, trainees may have no in-depth exposure to the specific and often sophisticated clinical techniques which can be used to work successfully with chronic patients and their families.

4. *Lack of Enough Clinical Exposure to Chronic Patients and Their Families:* In most training programs, clinical placements in "community psychiatry" are often short-term experiences in settings which are overextended, undersupervised, and unable to provide the highest quality of treatment. Trainees may even be encouraged to avoid chronic patients in these settings because they are not "good teaching cases." When trainees do see chronic patients, the trainees are often inadequately supervised and given too little encouragement to work with families and too little time to make a meaningful attachment to patient or family. In such placements, trainees are seldom able to develop a positive orientation toward clinical work with chronic patients, and may never be exposed to the possibility of providing chronic patients with high quality care.

5. *Lack of Specific Training in the Skills Needed for Working with Chronic Patients and Their Families:* These skills include: skill in sharing information with relatives; skill in teaching patients and their families about chronic mental illness; skill in developing specific approaches to such "management" problems faced by the families of the chronic mentally ill as denial of illness, bizarre behavior, and medication noncompliance; skill in utilization and development of the full range of community resources for patients and families; and skill in using systems coordination, interdisciplinary integration, and case consultation

to develop comprehensive and practical treatment plans. These skills are teachable—given adequate supervision and adequate exposure to a range of clinical situations—but they are rarely taught. Thus, since few training programs provide student professionals with the skills to work adequately with chronic patients and families, it is not surprising that so many of our families echo the complaint that a "good psychiatrist is hard to find."

Lack of Community Support

Most professionals working with chronic patients and families lack support both from within the mental health profession and from the outside community system. Despite the fact that the chronic mentally ill are the sickest, neediest, and most difficult patients, clinicians usually get little credit, status, or prestige from developing expertise with this population. In the majority of communities and training centers, the most esteemed clinicians concentrate their private office practices on the "less ill." Status in many academic centers is derived from research on mental illness (usually psychopharmacologic) but not from clinical skills with patients and families. So clinical work with the sickest patients is accorded the lowest prestige (Stern & Minkoff, 1979: Mirabi et al., 1985), and avoidance of clinical involvement with chronic patients and families is subtly encouraged.

Furthermore, clinicians, just like patients and families, are continually frustrated by inadequacies in the mental health care system. In most communities the system does not provide: (a) adequate 24-hour crisis back-up for their patients; (b) adequate supervised housing or day treatment programs; (c) adequate access to hospitalization; both because of lack of beds for chronic patients and because of the legal barriers to involuntary treatment; (d) adequate support by the social security and welfare systems, which often results in inordinate amounts of unreimbursed clinician time spent in advocating patient rights; (e) adequate financial reimbursement for their work with chronic patients, who often have insufficient third-party coverage such as Medicaid and Medicare and for their work with families, for whom many important services such as psychoeducational groups may be non-reimbursable. Overcoming affective barriers and training deficits, therefore, is only a beginning; without community support, the problem will continue.

In this chapter we have presented evidence for our belief that many families of chronically mentally ill patients living at home are critical of mental health professionals for not responding adequately to their needs and concerns. We have discussed some possible reasons for this failure to respond including: strong emotional reactions to chronic patients and their families which create barriers to successful intervention; serious training deficits in the skills necessary for successful intervention; and lack of peer validation or community support for working with this population. In the concluding chapter, we will make some recommendations for addressing these difficulties, and will discuss how we, as mental health professionals, can be more responsive to the families of the chronically mentally ill.

5

WHAT CAN BE DONE?

In the preceding chapters we have tried as much as possible to let the letters from the families speak for themselves. These letters eloquently portray the problems families face when caring for a chronically mentally ill family member. They recount the shock of the initial onset of mental illness; the anxiety, fear, anger, guilt, and sadness that accompany the awareness of the seriousness of the illness; the pain and misery of coping with bizarre behavior on a daily basis; the disruption of family relationships for all family members; the frustration of dealing with the legal system and the mental health system; and the difficulty of finding a good psychiatrist to provide appropriate care and support to all family members.

The following powerful statement summarizes these issues through one family's experience. It represents, however, many other families who believe that their cases have been mishandled by the mental health profession.

> . . . To add to all of the distress and pain that we experience having a mentally ill relative is the familiar experience of being isolated by mental health professionals from a cooperative role in helping our relative. Questions about the illness, the treatment plan and the prognosis, when answered, were answered only in a perfunctory manner. In the name of retaining confidentiality, telephone calls and letters frequently remained unanswered. It was such a frustrating expe-

rience because without help from the treating professional we had to give support to our son without the necessary tools.

Far more damaging, however, are what I call the more malevolent aspects of our experience as a family with mental health professionals. The damaging judgments made about our part in the cause and the exacerbation of the illness left each of us angry with the professionals and with each other. Our certainty about our love for our son and our concern for his welfare were shaken too often by the thoughtless criticism made by authoritative professionals. We began to internalize much of the expressed and implied criticism, giving credence to their perceptions and negating our perceptions, our own common sense, and our beliefs.

When I look back I am not surprised that we reacted that way. What else could we have done with little or no experience with the mental illness? They were the experts; we were a confused family of non-experts. We were a family struggling to keep our sanity amidst conflicting opinions and bizarre and frightening behavior on the part of our previously healthy son. It would have taken a much better informed and skeptical family than we were at the time to reject out of hand most of the preposterous judgments and recommendations.

The worst of it all was advice that was worthless because it did not consider the realities of the ways in which we functioned as a family and the values we held as individuals. Advice based on the belief that our son was manipulative and we were permissive was often poor advice because it was a simplistic evaluation of complex human interactions and situations. I was incapable of "closing the door" on my flagrantly psychotic son when he appeared at our door at 2 A.M., in the middle of a Chicago winter, wearing summer clothing and showing obvious signs of not have eaten or slept in several days. My worst fears—putting aside the inhumane act of closing a door on a sick individual—was that something terrible would happen to him because of his thought disorder and his physical state of decompensation. That fear was not an unrealistic one. The newspapers confirmed that when the background on the Hinckley case became public information. As a caring individual, I should have taken him into the house, fed him and helped put him to bed before calling a doctor for medication. That's what I would have done with any other sick person. But the advice that had been sternly handed down to my husband and myself by the professionals was what we followed instead.

That moment—the darkest moment in my life—signaled the end of complicity with professionals who viewed the family as cause and the behavior of the sick son only as self-induced and deviant. What we needed was support in what we were doing. What we also needed (and what we never received in the first trying years of my son's illness) was validation of us as a loving family, interested in helping the professional in treating and supporting our mentally ill relative. It was only when our common sense returned and when we began to demand that from professionals, and began to seek professionals who could provide it, that we began to work collaboratively with them to help our son. By that time we were informed consumers, but we were also a family battered by our experience.

How can this suffering be alleviated?

In this concluding chapter we will take our turn to speak. First we will summarize some of our thinking about meeting the needs of both families and patients, about educational approaches, and about self-help groups. Then we will draw from the emotional impact of the letters and our own professional backgrounds to formulate conclusions and recommendations about how we, as psychiatrists, can respond to the message that these letters convey.

Meeting the Needs of Both Families and Patients

Working with the chronically mentally ill means not only treating the patient but being the psychiatrist for the whole family, in a sense the "family psychiatrist." The gratification of playing such a role can be enormous as we get to know the family over a period of years and even decades, and as we become the trusted friend to whom all can turn at times of crises caused by the patient's illness.

To fulfill the role of "family psychiatrist," we need to convey a caring attitude to the family as well as to the patient and we need to be there whenever we are needed. The availability of a caring and wise physician or other mental health professional is especially appreciated when the family settles down for the "long haul," and the patient's illness becomes a permanent element of everyday life, when the possibility of a sudden shocking development shadows all attempts at future planning, when unpredicted or predictable acts of destructive or violent behavior shatter hopes and fuel anew helpless rage, and when loving concerns for the patient conflict with wishes to be liberated from the never-ending sorrows and fears.

We have seen in Chapter 4 that helpful advice on the practical management of the mentally ill is often difficult for relatives to obtain from professionals. Mental health professionals often avoid the issue entirely when asked for advice (Creer & Wing, 1974)—and when they do give advice it is often not helpful. For example, professionals, thinking they are being empathic with the problems of relatives, sometimes advise, "If the patient behaves badly, throw him out and lock the door after him so he cannot get back in." They do not realize that this could be a dangerous course of action for the patient and a guilt-provoking act beyond the capabilities of the relative. Still another example, "Forget about him and live your life," is easy to say but difficult, if not impossible, to do when the relative combines love and guilt in his feelings about a chronically mentally ill relative.

We will have to learn more about the practical management of the severely mentally ill at home and to be more forthcoming in offering advice to relatives on ways of dealing with mental illness. We need to use the practical advice that is available for families and that can be extremely helpful. The relatives' goals should be realistic; professionals and relatives together should first determine what can realistically be achieved. Then they can apply pressure to counteract the patients' social withdrawal, being careful not to push the patient towards standards beyond his capability, and leaving him a good deal of control over what he actually does.

Relatives can be helped to understand that social withdrawal may be a necessary defense for schizophrenics but that too much withdrawal may lead to a form of institutionalism in the homes, so that a balance must be struck. Although many families can learn this technique by trial and error over a period of years, it is often acquired only at great emotional cost that might have been avoided if they had been assisted by knowledgeable professionals. As another example of practical advice, relatives can be helped to see that although it may be useless to contradict delusional ideas, a patient can be told not to talk back to hallucinations in public.

A crucial time to deal sensitively with relatives is when the patient's first psychotic break occurs. *At that time relatives need to be told that current thinking is that the major psychoses result from a variety of etiological factors and are no longer considered to be primarily the result of "environmental factors," a term that most parents take to mean "bad" parenting.* It may be helpful to point out that there are genetic and hereditary factors in the etiology of mental illness. For some relatives this information reduces their guilt, relieves them of their fears that by their actions they will drive their other children crazy, and makes them more willing to cooperate with the patient's treatment. On the other hand, other families may well feel guilty about passing on a potential genetic predisposition to subsequent generations or the parents may blame each other. The professional's familiarity with the particular family and his skill in assessing their attitudes and anticipating their reactions can help him present this information in the most constructive way.

Families want basic information about the nature of the illness, its expectable course, and its long-range outlook. The information should be offered in simple language free of professional jargon. If an answer is not known, an honest admission of the limits of our knowledge is preferable to evasiveness, vagueness, or silence.

So, although "labeling" the patient as someone with a serious illness is a controversial issue, it has advantages that may outweigh its disadvantages. When a patient is behaving in a deeply disturbing way, the family is more likely to be able to help and support if they know the patient is ill rather than hostile or lazy (Anderson, Hogerty, & Reiss, 1981). Professionals who sincerely try to avoid "labeling" a patient by concealing the diagnosis may cause confusion and resentment; the family feels talked down to and left out of the treatment plan and procedures. The family that is excluded from treatment decisions, especially when these decisions affect them, feels powerless and angry and may undermine the treatment plan.

At the time of the first psychotic break, or later during crises requiring hospitalization, mental health professionals can reduce the trauma to the family by assisting in admission procedures and by explaining hospital policies and relevant mental health laws. Perhaps even more traumatic is the time of a patient's release from the hospital; it should be planned for with the family far in advance of the date of discharge, and aftercare arrangements should be fully discussed. Though many psychiatrists delegate aftercare planning to social caseworkers, the close collaboration of the psychiatrists themselves with patient, family, and institutional and community professionals is crucial to an effective outcome.

Professionals should be aware that a patient's illness can, and often does, strain the marriage of the parents to the breaking point. Being alert to this risk, relieving the guilt of the parents, and discouraging them from blaming each other for the illness can reduce the risk of breaking up the marriage. We need to help parents lower their expectations for their children and accept both the illness and a level of functioning far below their original aspirations. We should help them deal with their grieving and their feelings of sorrow, guilt, and anger; we should help them to respond appropriately to the patient's needs; and we should encourage them to feel they are partners in our treatment efforts, which will relieve to some extent their sense of helplessness. Ultimately, many families can reach a point of acceptance and can come to terms with living with mental illness. In this context, *families often need our help in setting realistic expectations not only for the patient but for themselves as well.*

An Educational Approach

The members of each family need and want specific knowledge about their relative's illness and what they can do about it. *Fortunately there is a growing willingness of professionals to impart specific information about, and ways of dealing with, mentally ill relatives.*

An important part of this information concerns medication. Because most patients are ambivalent about taking medication, and because families can impede or facilitate this process, families should be given information that may help them to support the medication regimen. This information may include statistics to demonstrate the high correlation between medication compliance and community tenure. The mechanisms of action and the main effects and possible side effects of antipsychotic medication, including tardive dyskinesia and weight gain, have to be given special attention. The use of anti-parkinsonian agents should also be explained, along with the need for ongoing feedback to the therapist about the effects of both types of drugs on the patient. The well-informed family can alert the physician about early signs of serious side effects or signals of impending exacerbation of the illness requiring an adjustment of the medication and other intervention.

The family of a schizophrenic patient, as well as the patient, needs to recognize that the illness includes a vulnerability to the interpersonal stresses common to everyday life. With this understanding, professionals can focus on helping the family identify the problems presenting the greatest threat to the patient's current and future stability (Goldstein & Kopeikin, 1981). The family can then be helped to develop strategies to avoid these stressful situations or to cope with them when the stresses cannot be avoided. This concrete, problem-focused, relatively simple format is particularly suited to the limited capacities of acute schizophrenics in the early stages of restitution. This approach is important because of the high relapse rate and stress of the first months after hospitalization. To improve the long-term benefits of therapy, treatment should probably progress beyond this focus on crisis and the management of imminent stresses.

Relatives should be told not always to be at the patient's beck and call (Berkowitz et al., 1981). That does not mean that dependency needs should not be gratified when appropriate and that adult schizophrenic children must always be "independent" and live away from home. The family is told implicitly or explicitly, however, that they should begin to lead an independent and satisfying life and that being totally self-sacrificing is counterproductive. Families are also encouraged to pay a normal amount of attention to the needs of other family members (Anderson, Hogarty, Reiss, 1981), since failure to do so is likely to deplete family resources and thus make long-term support of the patient increasingly difficult. Parallels are drawn between the course of schizophrenia and other chronic illnesses, such as diabetes, in which patients and families must learn ongoing management techniques and methods of living with the illness without allowing its symptoms to dominate their lives.

Schizophrenics have an abnormal sensitivity to environmental stimulation (Anderson, Hogarty, & Reiss, 1981). They seem to have cognitive deficits that make it difficult to process and respond to even normal amounts of environmental stimuli. In some families, overstimulation may lead patients to experience more disturbed behavior and psychotic symptoms. The work of a British group of mental health professionals suggests that the level of "expressed emotions" in families has a substantial relationship to the patient's level of functioning and likelihood of relapse. This work has led to a number of productive research hypotheses and offers promising new treatment approaches (Brown, Birley & Wing, 1972; Falloon, Boyd & McGill, 1984). For example, families are given ways in which they can create barriers to overstimulation by setting reasonable limits, having realistic goals, and allowing for interpersonal distance without rejection. In general, the family is encouraged to set limits on unreasonable, bizarre behavior before tension builds or blowups occur. The need for limits is stressed because many families feel that, since the patient is sick, he or she cannot be asked or expected to perform on any level. Creating a low-key environment does not mean creating a completely permissive one; for the person who is disorganized, structure is reassuring.

Families are encouraged to respect interpersonal boundaries in concrete ways—allowing family members to speak for themselves, permitting family members to do things separately, and recognizing each other's limitations and vulnerabilities. Both patient and family are helped to see that the need for distance relates to survival and does not constitute rejection. A family routine is encouraged that includes "time outs," which allow the patient or other family members to retreat to their rooms or go for a walk when feelings of agitation or overstimulation arise. Furthermore, patient and family are asked to discuss and agree on signals that indicate the need for psychological space and the need for support.

Many more psychiatrists and mental health professionals would be willing and able to help families if professional training programs would bring the problems of families to the attention of students and familiarize the latter with such approaches as the educational techniques just described. Clearly, these techniques benefit not only the families, but the patients as well. The respondents in our letters asked over and over for guidance in how to deal with such issues as a patient's unwillingness to cooperate with the treatment program by refusing to take medication as prescribed or by balking at attending scheduled interviews, group sessions or day treatment; unwillingness to comply with minimum standards of personal hygiene; unconcern about the needs of relatives in the home; disturbing the sleep of others by loudly playing the television, radio or record player all night; refusing to get out of bed; embarrassing the family by bizarre conduct and so interfering with the family's social life; becoming withdrawn and mute or apathetic; and threatening or actually engaging in suicidal or destructive behavior. For all these situations, families need to develop coping strategies. Professionals can learn a great deal about ways to deal with these problems from a growing number of books published for families, patients and professionals (see Bibliography).

Counseling should also include information about community resources and proper referral. Holden and Lewine (1982) found in a survey of families of chronically mentally ill individuals that "professionals were least helpful in directing (families) toward community resources." Professionals should maintain a regularly updated file on resources, listing specific contact persons. A personal call by a professional often facilitates the family's negotiation with the bureaucratic system.

Self-help Groups

In recent years families throughout the United States and other countries have begun to look to one another for support in order to overcome their sense of isolation and pool their experience and resources. They gain strength from the realization that others have successfully coped with similar problems. They are fighting the stigma of mental illness by publicly revealing that they are relatives of a mentally ill person. They lobby for more favorable legislation and better funding of mental health projects. These courageous people have "come out of the closet" where they used to hide to conceal the "shame" of mental illness in their family. Various local groups are affiliated with the National Alliance for the Mentally Ill. These groups have had a very beneficial effect on their members and they are gaining visibility in their efforts to improve the mental health system.

Professionals should be aware that family organizations are an important resource in the overall treatment of the chronically mentally ill and in helping families cope with the illness. Families of patients should be referred to an existing group or encouraged to form a local chapter where no such group exists. Professionals should also join such groups, attend the meetings and read the newsletters. The groups provide excellent postgraduate education for those of us who had no formal training on home care of the chronically mentally ill, problems these families face, and ways they have found to cope with them. A respectful participation in the self-help movement can do much to restore our somewhat tarnished image in the community and demonstrate to our patients as well as to their families that we truly care.

Conclusions and Recommendations

1. **Families, not just patients, need help.** As one of the letter writers put it: "Mental illness is indeed a family affair." No one in the family can remain unaffected by the mental illness of one of its members.

In this era of deinstitutionalization, relatives have become the real "primary care" agents for a large proportion of the severely and chronically mentally ill. But despite the large numbers of patients living with families, attention has only recently been turned to the problems of dealing with chronic mentally ill patients at home.

2. **As mental health professionals, we should provide the help that families need.** Relatives must learn to live with and deal with unpredictable behavior, never knowing how the patient will react to a particular situation, even to the point of occasional violence. Relatives may have to cope with the patient's lack of conversation, often an acute problem for a spouse who depends on the patient for companionship. Relatives may need our help to come to terms with the patient's social withdrawal, underactivity, excessive sleeping, or socially embarrassing behavior. If the patient and relatives stay together, in time they may reach an equilibrium that enables the patient to live outside a hospital but at the expense of restricting the lives of the family. Often relatives cannot leave the house even to go shopping without getting someone to watch the patient. So the relatives may not only become like jailers, but, in effect, be in jail themselves. To bear this imprisonment, or to find less restrictive alternatives for themselves, families need the ongoing help and support that only mental health professionals have had the training and experience to provide.

3. We need to overcome barriers within our professions to provide the help families need. As we saw in Chapter 4, many of our letter writers indicate that the help they need is often neither adequately nor willingly provided. The impression that many health professionals are reluctant to work with their patients' families is reported over and over again in our letters and is confirmed in some surveys.

In Chapter 4 we discussed some of the reasons why this phenomenon may have occurred. Although the trend now seems to be changing towards greater collaboration, some professionals still believe that only they are responsible for their patients. Some professionals fear that their patients will regard any contact with their families as a betrayal of confidentiality and will therefore lose trust in them. For psychoanalytically-oriented professionals, this attitude may stem from the view that seeing a patient's relatives may "contaminate" the transference, although, ironically, Sigmund Freud never hesitated to meet the relatives of his patients. This attitude may also have its roots in the biomedical model which locates the illness in the individual and therefore focuses all therapeutic interventions on the patient's person.

Our contention, however, is that the reluctance of professionals to interact with the family is primarily due to the fact that most mental health professionals have not been taught how to help families cope with their problems, while maintaining a positive and trusting relationship with the patient. When these specific skills are applied, the potential conflict between providing information to the family and betraying the patient's confidentiality can often be successfully resolved.

4. As mental health professionals, we have to learn to listen to families and to be aware that they may face a lifelong problem. The very act of empathic listening as well as our demonstration of respect for relatives as partners in our

efforts to help the patient can build the morale of a battered
family and bolster their courage and strength. An occasional
home visit not only provides the therapist with information
and insight which may be essential for appropriate treatment
planning and case management, but indicates to the family
that the caregiver is genuinely interested in helping them.
To help them we have to understand the tremendous problems of each phase of the illness: the initial shock of seeing
illness and irrationality in a relative; the giving up of aspirations for a chronically and severely ill child; the stress
of the illness on the marriage of parents or on the spouse
of a mentally ill person; and the disruption of the lives of
siblings.

**5. As mental health professionals, we must be extremely
careful to provide families with support rather than to blame
them.** Many schools of psychiatric thought have blamed the
patients' families for aggravating and even for causing the
patients' illnesses (Appleton, 1974). These views have always
been controversial, and currently are given less credence
than they were a few years ago. Furthermore, when professionals communicate these views to families, they forget that
being the relative of a mentally ill person is already traumatic
and often overwhelming (Lamb, 1982).

Even before its contact with the mental health establishment, the family is usually guilt-ridden and feels a keen
sense of failure for having "produced" a mentally ill child.
Professionals must be aware of this feeling and of the
additional impact of a parent's receiving a label like "schi-
zophrenogenic mother."

Even the concept of the "identified patient"—the idea
that the entire family is ill and the patient is simply the
person who has been labeled as the sick one—can add
further trauma. To the parents it can mean not only that
they have driven their child crazy but that the whole family
is sick as well. Thus, professionals must be careful not to

contribute to the burdens already borne by families of chronically mentally ill patients. Instead, the family needs to be relieved of their guilt as a first step toward beginning to cope.

The following comment illustrates the growing awareness of this point of view among family therapists: "The task of the therapist, first and foremost, is to understand and share the pain of the parents and other family members that results from the predicament in which they find themselves. That is a precondition to a therapeutic alliance and to helping them to function more adaptively. Too often family therapists . . . have worked in ways that implicitly and even explicitly blamed the family. Often families deal with the patient the way they do because they do not know how to cope with mental illness in any other way. They have never been told otherwise. That is why psychoeducational approaches to the family seem extraordinarily helpful. And insofar as group meetings with other parents are available, they afford the opportunity to share one's experience with others, to know that one is not alone, and to learn from other parents how to cope better" (Grunebaum, 1984).

6. As mental health professionals, we need to readjust our goals with families of chronic patients in order to take into account the biological determinants of mental illness. Based on our clinical experience, and our analysis of the available evidence, we believe that the major chronic mental illnesses are largely biologically determined. Although psychodynamic and familial factors contribute to the emergence and course of illness, they are not sufficient by themselves to *cause* illness. We believe, therefore, that once the course of the illness has been determined to be chronic, treatment interventions with patients and families are most effectively focused on facilitating adaptation to illness over time, rather than on futile and discouraging attempts to achieve "cure." We usually tell families explicitly that there are no scientific

data to suggest that serious mental illness is caused by childhood upbringing or family interaction (Falloon et al., 1981) and we outline biochemical and genetic theories in a manner comprehensible to the families.

7. As mental health professionals, we need to make sure that there are specific training programs in all our disciplines so that our trainees will learn the special skills necessary to deal effectively with the chronically mentally ill and their families. In Chapter 4, we described the specific deficits in this area on most current training programs. The necessary components of an effective training program for working with chronic mental illness have already been well described in the literature (Neilsen, Stein & Talbott, 1981). All the mental health professions need to make sure that their training programs include these components so that their graduates will be competent to provide the families of the chronic mentally ill with high quality care.

8. As mental health professionals, we need to take action to make care of the chronically mentally ill the highest priority of the public sector of mental health care. Relatives of the severely and chronically mentally ill have been frustrated and bitterly disappointed with every part of the public mental health system. Families are now organizing at the local, state, and national levels and are now reminding us more and more forcefully when we have been insensitive to the needs of both the severely mentally ill and their families. And as time goes on, we will be increasingly affected and held accountable by these relatives' groups.

Families are often bewildered by the priorities of many in the mental health system. They ask, and rightly so, whether the highest priority of public mental health should not be to serve the severely and chronically mentally ill? They cannot understand why the chronically mentally ill have so often been given low priority in community mental health programs. They have been frustrated to discover that when considerable sums of money have been made available for community mental health, community programs have often used these funds for everything but the chronically mentally ill. They have often been appalled at this reluctance to fund treatment and rehabilitation programs that meet the needs of long-term patients.

No one has been more affected by deinstitutionalization than families. A large proportion of the discharged patients have returned to families and, since deinstitutionalization, families have had to deal with their relatives' mental illness from the outset with only brief intermittent periods of hospitalization. As Hatfield, Farrell & Starr (1984) have observed, the mental health establishment has done an about-face and now turns to families as the primary resource— and sometimes the only resource—for a large proportion of the mentally ill. "We have a new/old panacea for treating the mentally ill: Return to the pre-asylum days and let families do it." Many families can and want to take on this responsibility, but can only do so if there are adequate supports and resources available. We need to help them make sure that these adequate supports and resources are available. We need to do all in our power to help *families to have ready access to good medication management, to receive sound advice on the everyday problems of living with a severely mentally ill person, and to have ready access to crisis intervention and hospitalization, day treatment, respite care and a full range of housing arrangements that will give them the assurance that there are alternatives if the situation becomes intolerable.*

9. As mental health professionals, we need to collaborate with families to bring about appropriate changes in the legal system so that involuntary treatment can be instituted when mental illness deprives patients of their ability to make rational judgments about their treatment and everyday lives. The problems created by restrictive commitment laws complicate

still further a painful process for the family. Most families find that only with great difficulty can they bring themselves to initiate commitment proceedings in the first place.

We have commented earlier about the problems that families have with the legal system. They have found that giving absolute priority to the civil rights of the mentally ill over their health and welfare is easy when one has power without responsibility, but can have devastating consequences. For instance, mental health lawyers can simply walk out of the courtroom and leave the havoc they have wrought by denying the protection of involuntary care to be dealt with by families and clinicians. Commitment procedures need to be less long and cumbersome, considering that the situations being dealt with are explosive and potentially dangerous.

A Final Word

We have some of the answers about chronic mental illness but there is still a vast amount to be learned. Just as in many conditions in other branches of medicine, we cannot cure. But we can alleviate pain and suffering and we can offer some solutions—not only for the mentally ill but also for their families. First, however, we must admit our limitations—to them and to ourselves. We must learn to listen to families as well as to patients; we must have realistic expectations; we must make ourselves available to families, although of course in ways which will not compromise our relationship with patients. We must try to maintain continuity of care with both patients and families and often see the therapeutic relationship as a lifelong one. Then we will find that we have formed a powerful partnership with families, both for treating the patients and for effective advocacy to increase vitally needed treatment, rehabilitation, and housing resources for the chronically mentally ill.

APPENDIX A: BIBLIOGRAPHY

Books for psychiatrists to recommend to family members (after they've read them themselves).

Guides

Arieti, S. *Understanding and Helping the Schizophrenic: A Guide for Family and Friends.* New York: Simon & Schuster, 1979.

Bernheim, K.F., & Lewine, R.J.R. *Schizophrenia: Symptoms, Causes, Treatments.* New York: Norton, 1979.

Bernheim, K.F., Lewine, R.J.R., & Beale, C.T. *The Caring Family: Living with Chronic Mental Illness.* New York: Random House, 1982.

Bowers, M. *Retreat from Sanity. The Structure of Emerging Psychosis.* New York: Human Sciences Press, 1974.

Falloon, I., Boyd, J., & McGill, C. *Family Care for Schizophrenia: A Problem Solving Approach to Mental Illness.* New York: Guilford Press, 1984.

Hatfield, A. *Coping with Mental Illness in the Family: A Family Guide.* Washington, DC: The National Alliance for the Mentally Ill, 1985.

Kline, N.S. *From Sad to Glad.* New York: Ballantine, 1974.

Kanter, J.S. *Coping Strategies for Relatives of the Mentally Ill.* Washington, DC: The National Alliance for the Mentally Ill, 1984.

Park, C.C., & Shapiro, L. *You Are Not Alone: Understanding and Dealing With Mental Illness, A Guide for Patients, Families, Doctors, and Other Professionals.* Boston: Little, Brown, 1976.

Schou, M. *Lithium Treatment of Manic-Depressive Illness: A Practical Guide.* Basel: Karger, 1983.

Seeman, M.V., Littmann, S.K., Plummer, E. et al. *Living and Working With Schizophrenia.* Toronto: University of Toronto Press, 1982.

Torrey, F.F. *Surviving Schizophrenia: A Family Manual.* New York: Harper & Row, 1983.

Tsuang, M.T. *Schizophrenia: The Facts.* New York: Harper and Row, 1983.

Vine, P. *Families in Pain: Children, Siblings, Spouses, and Parents of the Mentally Ill Speak Out.* New York: Pantheon Books, 1982.

Wasow, M. *Coping With Schizophrenia: A Survival Manual for Parents, Relatives and Friends.* Palo Alto: Science & Behavior Books, 1982.

First-hand Accounts

Beers, C. *A Mind That Found Itself.* Pittsburgh: Pittsburgh Univ Press, 1981.

Benzinger, B.F. *A Prison Of My Mind.* New York: Walker, 1981.

Fair, T.D. *Lily.* Denver: Accent Books, 1982.

Knauth, P. *Operators and Things.* New York: New American Library, 1976.

Plath, S. *The Bell Jar.* New York: Harper & Row, 1971.

Sheehan, S. *Is There No Place On Earth For Me?* Boston: Houghton Mifflin, 1982.

Wechsler, J.A. *In a Darkness.* New York: Norton, 1972.

APPENDIX B: RESOURCE INFORMATION

For the address of your local family support group contact:

National Alliance for the Mentally Ill
1901 N. Fort Myer Drive, Suite 500
Arlington, VA 22209

For information on local resources available to help a mentally ill person contact:

National Mental Health Association
1021 Prince Street
Alexandria, Virginia 22314

For further information and materials available about mental illness contact:

National Institute of Mental Health Clearing House
Rockville, Maryland

REFERENCES

Anderson, C.M., Hogarty, G., & Reiss, D.J. The psychoeducational family treatment of schizophrenia. In M.J. Goldstein (Ed.). *New Directions for Mental Health Services: New Developments in Interventions with Families of Schizophrenics*, no. 12. San Francisco: Jossey-Bass, 1981.

Appleton, W.S. Mistreatment of patients' families by psychiatrists. *American Journal of Psychiatry*, 131(6):655–657, 1974.

Berkowitz, R., Kuipers, L., Eberlein-Frief, R., & Leff, T. Lowering expressed emotion in relatives of schizophrenics. In J.J. Goldstein (Ed.), *New Directions for Mental Health Services: New Developments in Interventions with Families of Schizophrenics*, no. 12. San Francisco: Jossey-Bass, 1981.

Brown, G.W., Birley, J.L.T., & Wing, J.K. Influence of family life on the course of schizophrenic disorders: A replication. *British Journal of Psychiatry*, 121:241–58, 1972.

Cadoret, R.J. Evidence for Genetic Inheritance of Primary Affective Disorder in Adoptees. *American Journal of Psychiatry*, 135:463–466, 1978.

Creer, C., & Wing, J.K. *Schizophrenia at Home*. London: National Schizophrenia Fellowship, 1974.

Falloon, I., Boyd, J., & McGill, C. *Family Care for Schizophrenia: A Problem Solving Approach to Mental Illness*. New York: Guilford Press, 1984.

Falloon, I.R.H., Boyd, J.L., McGill, C.W., Strang, J.S., & Moss, H.B. Family management training in the community care of schizophrenia. In M.J. Goldstein (Ed.), *New Directions for Mental Health Services: New Developments in Interventions with Families of Schizophrenics*, no. 12. San Francisco: Jossey-Bass, 1981.

Goldstein, M.J., & Kopeikin, H.S. Short-and long-term effects of combining drug and family therapy. In M.J. Goldstein (Ed.), *New Directions for Mental Health Services: New Developments in Interventions with Families of Schizophrenics*, no. 12. San Francisco: Jossey-Bass, 1981.

Gottesman, I.I., & Shields, J. *Schizophrenia and Genetics: A Twin Study Vantage Point*. New York: Academic Press, 1972.

Grunebaum, H. Comments on Terkelson, K., Schizophrenia and the family: II. Adverse effects of family therapy. *Family Process*, (23):421–428, 1984.

Hatfield, A., Farrell, E., & Starr, S. The family's perspective on the homeless. In Homeless Mentally Ill. Washington, DC: American Psychiatric Press, 1984.

Holden, D.F., & Lewine, R.R. How families evaluate mental health professionals, resources and effects of illness. *Schizophrenia Bulletin,* NIMH 8(4):623–633, 1982.

Kety, S.S., Rosenthal, D., & Wender, P.H. Studies based on a total sample of adopted individuals and their relatives: Why they were necessary, what they demonstrated and failed to demonstrate. *Schizophrenia Bulletin,* 3:413–428, 1976.

Lamb, H.R. *Treating the long-term mentally ill: Beyond deinstitutionalization.* San Francisco: Jossey-Bass, 1982.

Lamb, H.R., & Goertzel, V. The long-term patient in the era of community treatment. *Archives of General Psychiatry,* 34(6):679–682, 1977.

Minkoff, K. A map of chronic mental patients. In J.A. Talbott (Ed.), *The Chronic Mental Patient.* Washington, DC: The American Psychiatric Association, 1978.

Mirabi, M., Weinman, M.L., & Magnetti, S.M. Professional attitudes toward the chronic mentally ill. *Hospital & Community Psychiatry,* 36:404–405, 1985.

Myerson, A.T. What are the barriers or obstacles to treatment and care of the chronically disabled mentally ill? In J.A. Talbott (Ed.), *The Chronic Mental Patient,* Washington, DC: American Psychiatric Association, 1978.

Neilsen, III, A.C., Stein, L.I., & Talbott, J.A. Encouraging psychiatrists to work with chronic patients: Opportunities and limitations of residency education. *Hospital & Community Psychiatry,* 32:767–775, 1981.

Rosenthal, D., Wender, P.H., Kety, S.S., Welner, J., & Schulsinger, F. The adopted away offspring of schizophrenics. *American Journal of Psychiatry,* 128:307–311, 1971.

Stern, R., & Minkoff, K. Paradoxes in programming for chronic patients in a community clinic. *Hospital & Community Psychiatry,* 30:613–617, 1979.

White, H., & Bennett, M. Training psychiatric residents in chronic care. *Hospital & Community Psychiatry,* 32:339–343, 1981.

GAP COMMITTEES AND MEMBERSHIP

COMMITTEE ON ADOLESCENCE
Silvio J. Onesti, Jr., Belmont,
  Mass.,
  Chairperson
Ian A. Canino, New York, N.Y.
Sherman C. Feinstein, Highland
  Park, Ill.
Warren J. Gadpaille, Denver,
  Colo.
Michael G. Kalogerakis, New
  York, N.Y.
Clarice J. Kestenbaum, New
  York, N.Y.
Derek Miller, Chicago, Ill.

COMMITTEE ON AGING
Gene D. Cohen, Rockville, Md.,
  Chairperson
Eric D. Caine, Rochester, N.Y.
Charles M. Gaitz, Houston, Tex.
Gabe J. Maletta, Minneapolis,
  Minn.
Robert J. Nathan, Philadelphia,
  Pa.
George H. Pollock, Chicago, Ill.
Kenneth M. Sakauye, Chicago,
  Ill.
Charles A. Shamoian, White
  Plains, N.Y.
F. Conyers Thompson, Jr.,
  Atlanta, Ga.

COMMITTEE ON CHILD
PSYCHIATRY
Theodore Shapiro, New York,
  N.Y.,
  Chairperson

Paul L. Adams, Galveston,
  Tex.
James M. Bell, Canaan, N.Y.
Harlow Donald Dunton, New
  York, N.Y.
Joseph Fischhoff, Detroit Mich.
Joseph M. Green, Madison,
  Wis.
John F. McDermott, Jr.,
  Honolulu, Hawaii
John Schowalter, New Haven,
  Conn.
Peter E. Tanguay, Los Angeles,
  Calif.
Lenore F.C. Terr, San Francisco,
  Calif.

COMMITTEE ON COLLEGE
STUDENTS
Kent E. Robinson, Towson, Md.,
  Chairperson
Robert L. Arnstein, Hamden,
  Conn.
Varda Backus, La Jolla, Calif.
Harrison P. Eddy, New York,
  N.Y.
Myron B. Liptzin, Chapel Hill,
  N.C.
Malkah Tolpin Notman,
  Brookline, Mass.
Gloria C. Onque, Pittsburgh, Pa.
Elizabeth Aub Reid, Cambridge,
  Mass.
Earle Silber, Chevy Chase, Md.
Tom G. Stauffer, White Plains,
  N.Y.

COMMITTEE ON CULTURAL
PSYCHIATRY
Ezra E.H. Griffith, New Haven,
Conn.,
Chairperson
Edward F. Foulks, Philadelphia,
Pa.
Pedro Ruiz, Houston, Tex.
John P. Spiegel, Waltham, Mass.
Ronald M. Wintrob, Providence,
R.I.
Joe Yamamoto, Los Angeles,
Calif.

COMMITTEE ON THE FAMILY
W. Robert Beavers, Dallas, Tex.,
Chairperson
Ellen M. Berman, Merrion, Pa.
Lee Combrinck-Graham,
Philadelphia, Pa.
Ira D. Glick, New York, N.Y.
Frederick Gottlieb, Los Angeles,
Calif.
Henry U. Grunebaum,
Cambridge, Mass.
Herta A. Guttman, Montreal,
Quebec
Judith Landau-Stanton,
Rochester, N.Y.
Ann L. Price, Hartford, Conn.
Lyman C. Wynne, Rochester,
N.Y.

COMMITTEE ON GOVERNMENTAL
AGENCIES
William W. Van Stone, Palo
Alto, Calif.,
Chairperson
James P. Cattell, San Diego,
Calif.
Sidney S. Goldensohn, New
York, N.Y.
Naomi Heller, Washington, D.C.
Roger Peele, Washington, D.C.

COMMITTEE ON HANDICAPS
Norman R. Bernstein, Chicago,
Ill.,
Chairperson
Meyer S. Gunther, Chicago, Ill.
William H. Sack, Portland, Oreg.
William A. Sonis, Minneapolis,
Minn.
George Tarjan, Los Angeles,
Calif.
Thomas G. Webster,
Washington, D.C.
Henry H. Work, Bethesda, Md.

COMMITTEE ON INTERNATIONAL
RELATIONS
Francis F. Barnes, Chevy Chase,
Md.,
Chairperson
Robert M. Dorn, Sacramento,
Calif.
John S. Kafka, Washington, D.C.
Edward Khantzian, Haverhill,
Mass.
John E. Mack, Chestnut Hill,
Mass.
Rita R. Rogers, Palos Verdes
Estates, Calif.
Bertram H. Schaffner, New
York, N.Y.
Stephen B. Shanfield, Tucson,
Ariz.
Vamik D. Volkan, Charlottesville,
Va.

COMMITTEE ON MEDICAL
EDUCATION
David R. Hawkins, Chicago, Ill.,
Chairperson
Gene Abroms, Ardmore, Pa.
Charles M. Culver, Hanover,
N.H.
Steven L. Dubovsky, Denver,
Colo.
Saul I. Harrison, Torrance, Calif.

Harold I. Lief, Philadelphia, Pa.
Carol Nadelson, Boston, Mass.
Carolyn B. Robinowitz,
Washington, D.C.
Stephen C. Scheiber, Tucson,
Ariz.
Sidney L. Werkman, Denver,
Colo.
Veva H. Zimmerman, New York,
N.Y.

COMMITTEE ON MENTAL HEALTH
SERVICES
George F. Wilson, Belle Mead,
N.J.,
Chairperson
Allan Beigel, Tucson, Ariz.
Merrill T. Eaton, Omaha, Nebr.
John M. Hamilton, Baltimore,
Md.
W. Walter Menninger, Topeka,
Kans.
Jose Maria Santiago, Tucson,
Ariz.
Herzl R. Spiro, Milwaukee, Wis.
William L. Webb, Jr., Hartford,
Conn.
Jack A. Wolford, Pittsburgh, Pa.

COMMITTEE ON PREVENTIVE
PSYCHIATRY
Stephen Fleck, New Haven,
Conn.,
Chairperson
Viola W. Bernard, New York,
N.Y.
Stanley I. Greenspan, Bethesda,
Md.
William H. Hetznecker,
Philadelphia, Pa.
Richard G. Morrill, Boston,
Mass.
Harris B. Peck, New Rochelle,
N.Y.
Naomi Rae-Grant, Hamilton,
Ontario

Anne Marie Wolf, Philadelphia,
Pa.

COMMITTEE ON PSYCHIATRY AND
LAW
Jonas R. Rappeport, Baltimore,
Md.,
Chairperson
Park E. Dietz, Charlottesville,
Va.
John Donnelly, Hartford, Conn.
Carl P. Malmquist, Minneapolis,
Minn.
Herbert C. Modlin, Topeka,
Kans.
Phillip J. Resnick, Cleveland,
Ohio
Loren J. Roth, Pittsburgh, Pa.
Joseph Satten, San Francisco,
Calif.
William D. Weitzel, Lexington,
Ky.
Howard V. Zonana, New Haven,
Conn.

COMMITTEE ON PSYCHIATRY AND
RELIGION
Albert J. Lubin, Woodside,
Calif.,
Chairperson
Sidney Furst, Bronx, N.Y.
Richard C. Lewis, New Haven,
Conn.
Earl A. Loomis, Jr., Augusta,
Ga.
Mortimer Ostow, Bronx, N.Y.
Sally K. Severino, White Plains,
N.Y.
Clyde R. Snyder, PSF, Calif.
Michael R. Zales, Greenwich,
Conn.

COMMITTEE ON PSYCHIATRY IN
INDUSTRY
Barrie S. Greiff, Cambridge,
Mass.,
Chairperson

William B. Hunter, III,
Albuquerque, N.M.
Roberto L. Jimenez, San
Antonio, Tex.
Melvin Sabshin, Washington,
D.C.

COMMITTEE ON THERAPY
Allan D. Rosenblatt, La Jolla,
Calif.,
Chairperson
Henry W. Brosin, Tucson, Ariz.
Eugene B. Feigelson, Brooklyn,
N.Y.
Robert Michels, New York, N.Y.
Andrew P. Morrison, Cambridge,
Mass.
William C. Offenkrantz,
Milwaukee, Wis.

CONTRIBUTING MEMBERS
John E. Adams, Gainesville, Fl.
Carlos C. Alden, Jr., Buffalo,
N.Y.

Eric A. Baum, Akron, Ohio
Spencer Bayles, Houston, Tex.
Aaron T. Beck, Wynnewood, Pa.
C. Christian Beels, New York,
N.Y.
Elissa P. Benedek, Ann Arbor,
Mich.
Sidney Berman, Washington,
D.C.
Wilfred Bloomberg, Cambridge,
Mass.
H. Keith H. Brodie, Durham,
N.C.
Charles M. Bryant, San
Francisco, Calif.
Ewald W. Busse, Durham, N.C.
Robert N. Butler, New York,
N.Y.

Eugene M. Caffey, Jr., Bowie,
Md.

Paul Chodoff, Washington, D.C.
Ian L.W. Clancey, Ontario,
Canada
Sanford I. Cohen, Boston, Mass.

James S. Eaton, Jr., Washington,
D.C.
Lloyd C. Elam, Nashville, Tenn.
Stanley H. Eldred, Belmont,
Mass.
Joseph T. English, New York,
N.Y.
Louis C. English, Pomona, N.Y.

Sherman C. Feinstein, Highland
Park, Ill.
Archie R. Foley, New York,
N.Y.
Daniel X. Freedman, Chicago,
Ill.

Alexander Gralnick, Port
Chester, N.Y.
Milton Greenblatt, Sepulveda,
Calif.
Lawrence F. Greenleigh, Los
Angeles, Calif.
Jon E. Gudeman, Lexington,
Mass.

Seymour L. Halleck, Chapel Hill,
N.C.
Stanley Hammons, Lexington,
Ky.
J. Cotter Hirschberg, Topeka,
Kans.

Jay Katz, New Haven, Conn.
James A. Knight, New Orleans,
La.
Othilda M. Krug, Cincinnati,
Ohio

Alan I. Levenson, Tucson, Ariz.
Ruth W. Lidz, Woodbridge,
Conn.
Orlando B. Lightfoot, Boston,
Mass.

Reginald S. Lourie, Chevy Chase, Md.

Norman L. Loux, Sellersville, Pa.

John A. MacLeod, Cincinnati, Ohio

Leo Madow, Philadelphia, Pa.

Charles A. Malone, Cleveland, Ohio

Peter A. Martin, Bloomfield Hills, Mich.

Ake Mattsson, New York, N.Y.

Alan A. McLean, Westport, Conn.

David Mendell, Houston, Tex.

Roy W. Menninger, Topeka, Kans.

Mary E. Mercer, Nyack, N.Y.

Joseph D. Noshpitz, Washington, D.C.

Charles P. O'Brien, Philadelphia, Pa.

Bernard L. Pacella, New York, N.Y.

Herbert Pardes, New York, N.Y.

Norman L. Paul, Lexington, Mass.

Marvin E. Perkins, Salem, Va.

Betty J. Pfefferbaum, Houston, Tex.

Charles A. Pinderhughes, Bedford, Mass.

David N. Ratnavale, Bethesda, Md.

W. Donald Ross, Cincinnati, Ohio

Lester H. Rudy, Chicago, Ill.

George E. Ruff, Philadelphia, Pa.

David S. Sanders, Los Angeles, Calif.

Donald J. Scherl, Brooklyn, N.Y.

Kurt O. Schlesinger, San Francisco, Calif.

Charles Shagass, Philadelphia, Pa.

Miles F. Shore, Boston, Mass.

Albert J. Silverman, Ann Arbor, Mich.

Benson R. Snyder, Cambridge, Mass.

David A. Soskis, Bala Cynwyd, Pa.

Jeanne Spurlock, Washington, D.C.

Brandt F. Steele, Denver, Colo.

Alan A. Stone, Cambridge, Mass.

Robert E. Switzer, Dunn Loring, Va.

Perry C. Talkington, Dallas, Tex.

Bryce Templeton, Philadelphia, Pa.

Prescott W. Thompson, Beaverton, Oreg.

Joe P. Tupin, Sacramento, Calif.

John A. Turner, San Francisco, Calif.

Gene L. Usdin, New Orleans, La.

Warren T. Vaughan, Jr., Portola Valley, Calif.

Andrew S. Watson, Ann Arbor, Mich.

Bryant M. Wedge, Washington, D.C.

Joseph B. Wheelwright, Kentfield, Calif.

Robert L. Williams, Houston, Tex.

Paul Tyler Wilson, Bethesda, Md.

Sherwyn M. Woods, Los Angeles, Calif.

Kent A. Zimmerman, Berkeley, Calif.

Israel Zwerling, Philadelphia, Pa.

LIFE MEMBERS

C. Knight Aldrich, Charlottesville, Va.

Bernard Bandler, Cambridge, Mass.
Walter E. Barton, Hartland, Vt.
Viola W. Bernard, New York, N.Y.
Murray Bowen, Chevy Chase, Md.
Henry W. Brosin, Tucson, Ariz.
John Donnelly, Hartford, Conn.
O. Spurgeon English, Narberth, Pa.
Dana L. Farnsworth, Boston, Mass.
Stephen Fleck, New Haven, Conn.
Jerome Frank, Baltimore, Md.
Robert S. Garber, Osprey, Fl.
Paul E. Huston, Iowa City, Iowa
Margaret M. Lawrence, Pomona, N.Y.
Harold I. Lief, Philadelphia, Pa.
Judd Marmor, Los Angeles, Calif.
Karl A. Menninger, Topeka, Kans.
Herbert C. Modlin, Topeka, Kans.
John C. Nemiah, Hanover, N.H.
Mabel Ross, Sun City, Ariz.
Julius Schreiber, Washington, D.C.
George Tarjan, Los Angeles, Calif.
Jack A. Wolford, Pittsburgh, Pa.
Henry H. Work, Bethesda, Md.

BOARD OF DIRECTORS

OFFICERS

President
Michael R. Zales
Edgewood Drive
Greenwich, Conn. 06830

President-Elect
Jerry M. Lewis
Timberlawn Hospital
P.O. Box 270789
Dallas, Tex. 75227

Secretary
Allan Beigel
30 Camino Español
Tuscon, Ariz. 85716

Treasurer
Charles B. Wilkinson
600 E. 22nd Street
Kansas City, Mo. 64108

Board Members

Roger Peele
John J. Schwab
John A. Talbott
Lenore F.C. Terr

Past Presidents
*William C. Menninger	1946–51
Jack R. Ewalt	1951–53
Walter E. Barton	1953–55
*Sol W. Ginsburg	1955–57
Dana L. Farnsworth	1957–59
*Marion E. Kenworthy	1959–61
Henry W. Brosin	1961–63
*Leo H. Bartemeier	1963–65
Robert S. Garber	1965–67
Herbert C. Modlin	1967–69
John Donnelly	1969–71
George Tarjan	1971–73
Judd Marmor	1973–75
John C. Nemiah	1975–77
Jack A. Wolford	1977–79
Robert W. Gibson	1979–81
*Jack Weinberg	1981–82
Henry H. Work	1982–85

* deceased